WORLD
CRAFTS

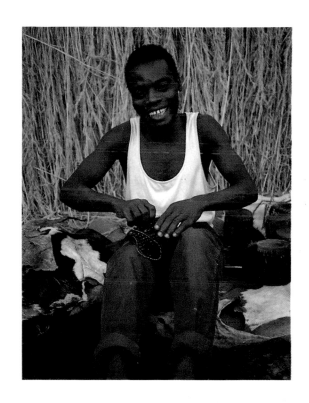

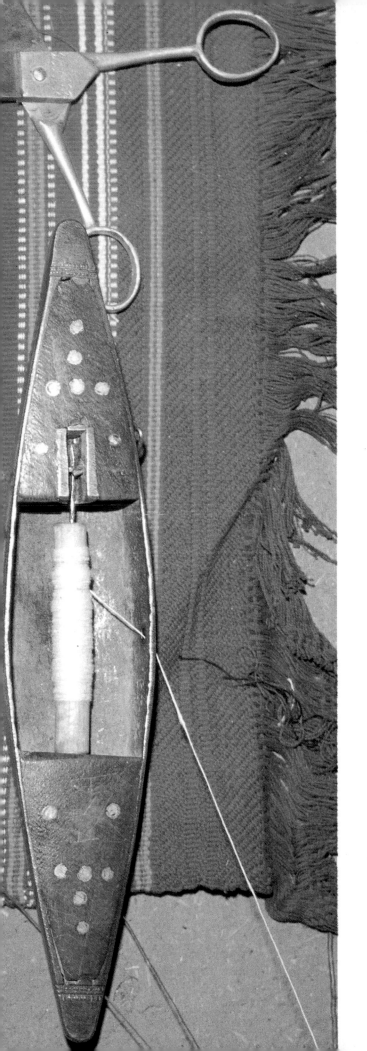

WORLD CRAFTS

A CELEBRATION OF DESIGNS AND SKILLS

JACQUELINE HERALD

Lark Books

OXFAM

Published in the United States in 1993 by
Lark Books
50 College Street
Asheville, NC, USA 28801

ISBN 0-937274-66-6

Library of Congress Cataloging-in-Publication Data
Herald, Jacqueline.
    World crafts / Jacqueline Herald.
        p.   cm.
    Includes index.
    ISBN 0-937274-66-6
    1. Handicraft–Developing countries.   I. Title
TT127.H47   1993
745'.09172'4–dc20   92-45890
                                                        CIP

10   9   8   7   6   5   4   3   2   1

First published in 1992 by
Charles Letts & Co Ltd
Letts of London House
Parkgate Road
London SW11 4NQ

Designed and edited by
Anness Publishing Ltd
Boundary Studios
1 Boundary Row
London SE1 8HP

Photographs © 1992
Oxfam Activities and individual
photographers as credited
Text © 1992 Jacqueline Herald

The right of Jacqueline Herald to be identified
as author of this work has been asserted by her
in accordance with the Copyright, Designs
and Patents Act 1988.

Editorial Director: Joanna Lorenz
Design styling: Peter Bridgewater
Layout design: Kit Johnson
Editorial assistant: Charles Moxham
Still-life photography: John Freeman
Oxfam Trading consultants: Rachel Wilshaw and Emma Gough

Printed and bound in Hong Kong

Page one: *Asafu Amini making a cow-hide drum in a village
near Lake Malawi, southern Africa.*
Page two: *Instruments for weaving traditional pattus
(a type of shawl) in the Thar desert of Rajasthan.*

CONTENTS

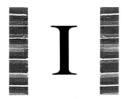 am delighted to be given the chance to present *World Crafts*, because, at last, the skills of the men and women who make crafts in developing countries are being celebrated. Most of the source information and all the photographs for this book have resulted from Oxfam Trading's programme of work with craft producers in Asia, Africa and Latin America, which we call "Bridge". Oxfam Trading is involved with craftspeople who are often vulnerable, living on the margins of their societies, and with little access to markets for their products and few opportunities to earn income in other ways. "Bridge" helps people increase their incomes through a programme of support and services which includes marketing crafts through the Oxfam Shops and catalogues in the UK. This book enables us, in "Bridge", to share information we have collected over many years.

I have been fortunate, during my work in the last nine years, in being able to visit craftspeople all over the world and to talk to them about their work. My abiding memory is of the pride people have in their skills. I remember meeting Ye-Ellen in a bamboo house on stilts on a mountain in Mindanao in the Southern Philippines, and the

ABOVE: *Monodai Mergan outlining the procedure for making dye from a mixture of dung and ground roots; Orissa, India.*

OPPOSITE: *Women working companionably together in the compound of SMM Theatre Crafts Trust on the outskirts of Delhi, India.*

care she took as she showed me how she made *t'nalak* cloth, describing and demonstrating all the processes in a couple of hours. Similarly, in a small town called Nowrangpur, in Orissa, India, four generations of one family – great-grandmother, grandmother, mother and daughter – sat down with me to describe how they made lacquer boxes and demonstrated on the spot how the lacquer is prepared. And in a village nearby, Monodai Mergan interrupted her work to tell me in the greatest detail how she prepared the natural dyes for colouring the yarn used by the local weavers.

Very few people have been as lucky as I have to find out at first hand how these crafts are made or who makes them. *World Crafts* gives you a glimpse into the lives of craftspeople all over the world, people who fashion beautiful, everyday things from the raw materials they find around them. It is an appreciation in words and pictures of cultures, traditions and skills which are vibrantly alive and well, surviving the depredations of the late 20th century. Above all, this book is a tribute to craftspeople. I hope you enjoy it!

Carol Wills
Head of Buying and Producer Services
Oxfam Trading

WORLD CRAFTS
AN INTRODUCTION

THIS BOOK PRESENTS AN OVERVIEW OF CRAFTS FROM DEVELOPING COUNTRIES
IN ASIA, AFRICA AND LATIN AMERICA. IN SO DOING, IT LOOKS AT THE PEOPLE
BEHIND THE PRODUCTS, AND THE CONTEXT IN WHICH THEY ARE PRACTISING
THEIR CRAFT. THE EMPHASIS IS ON WHAT IS HAPPENING TODAY, ALTHOUGH THE
HISTORY OF THE MAIN TECHNIQUES, THE USE OF MATERIALS, THE REASONS WHY
CERTAIN PRODUCTS WERE ORIGINALLY MADE, AND THE WORLD MARKET FOR
THESE CRAFTS ARE ALSO DISCUSSED.

During the last 20 years or so, interest in crafts has been growing and a wide range of books has been published on the subject. Many are specialized, focusing on a particular technique, or highlighting the work of named Western makers. Other books take a broader view, often featuring decorative images of non-Western crafts. However, these books usually lack one particular dimension: an insight into the lives of the makers, and why they produce their craft work. *World Crafts* sets out to redress this balance.

The chapters of this book are arranged according to the type of technique used, and their function. This gives the opportunity to juxtapose crafts which come from very different cultures, but which have been made for similar purposes. A fascinating aspect of the subject is that many techniques are common to people on opposite sides of the world, although their cultures may not have come directly into contact with one another.

In taking this approach it has been possible to bring out the basic factors which influence the

ABOVE: *Basketry hats being worn in an Indonesian market place.*

OPPOSITE: *Traditional basket 'raincoats' in Cameroon; they are designed to be used when bent double during agricultural work.*

OPPOSITE, BORDER: *Detail of leaf plate made in Bihar state, North India; the leaves are collected from the abundant forests around Chaibasa and pressed.*

character of the crafts: their purpose; the availability of raw materials; the method of construction and skill of the maker; and local and foreign influences on forms and decorative motifs.

WHY MAKE CRAFTS?

Crafts are much more than objects to be handled and admired. In countries in the West, most crafts are done as a leisure activity, but in the developing world, the main reason for making them is economic. Given that earnings from crafts are desperately low, this fact may seem difficult to accept. But when there is no alternative means of earning a cash income, people turn to craft production out of sheer necessity.

One of the most significant aspects of crafts, from the makers' points of view, is the way in which production can fit into the patterns of the working day and the seasons of the year. Many processes may be worked conveniently around domestic duties and the agricultural calendar. Many women in particular work their crafts in any spare moment of the day, which is otherwise filled with tasks such as looking after children, feeding animals, tending crops, and cooking.

ABOVE: *Peruvian potato crop. It is common in developing countries for people to live in the countryside, but to have no formal employment or land of their own. As paid agricultural work is seasonal, many people turn to crafts production at other times of the year.*

LEFT: *Income from crafts can make all the difference between poverty and dignity; this Bangladeshi woman had no money to buy a cow until she joined a jute crafts co-operative and began to save.*

In such circumstances, the skills required are often taken for granted and the maker's identity is not known beyond the family or immediate community. Producers may be making functional items such as cooking pots and baskets, blankets and quilts – for their own needs – or they may be employed within the informal sector of the economy (often termed "cottage industry"), producing crafts for sale. Their work is in marked contrast to that of master craftsmen who have undergone long apprenticeships. Such masters may enjoy the same status as artists in the West and the value of their work reflects this; they are in the minority, however, and are not the focus of this book.

Another major impetus for the production of crafts is their cultural significance. This is especially true of decorative pieces made expressly for important occasions such as marriage and religious festivals, at which they are worn, displayed or given as gifts. These may signify the status of the owner, and are usually treasured as family heirlooms. However, many communities also attach great importance to items in daily use, such as clothing, jewellery, carpets and cooking pots, which give them a strong sense of identity; examples include women's blouses from Guatemala; men's shawls from Rajasthan, India; tribal jewellery from Thailand; and ikat shoulder cloths from Sabu island, Indonesia.

CHANGING TRADITIONS

In the developing world during the last few decades, there has been a tremendous increase in the numbers of people turning to craft production in order to generate income. Increasingly,

In more remote parts of the world people still use natural materials to make everyday items with designs perfectly adapted to their purpose. A man carries a basketry coracle (LEFT); a T'Boli house-on-stilts in the Philippines is created from bamboo (RIGHT); and a basket is used for collecting cattle fodder in the Himalayas of Nepal (BELOW).

such production is not just a complementary or supplementary activity but the sole means of earning a living. This development is altering the character of crafts and their production.

Such change is not new. For as long as crafts have been made for sale, they have been adapted to suit the market. To give just one historical example, the hand-painted cotton chintzes of India were, by the late 17th century, being made to designs expressly sent out from Europe, and their use was changed from floorspreads to bedcurtains and coverlets.

One of the most important consequences (for the consumer) of the Industrial Revolution in Britain was that machine-imitations of handcrafted textiles became readily available. By the early 19th century centres such as Paisley, near Glasgow in Scotland, were mass-producing machine-made versions of hand-crafted textiles such as the highly prized shawls of Kashmir in India. This put extreme pressure on the Kashmiri shawl producers, who had become almost entirely dependent on the export market.

The Western factory system, which mechanized cottage industries, inevitably devalued hand skills. By the mid-19th century manual production was finding it difficult to compete with factory goods, which were so much cheaper than the traditional, hand-made item. But towards the end of the century, the Arts and Crafts Movement brought about a new appreciation of the hand-made product through the ideology of artists and designers such as William Morris. He greatly admired the designs and skills put into Middle Eastern carpets and Indian block-printed textiles. These were naturally dyed rather than brightly coloured with synthetic dyestuffs, and

ABOVE: *A powerloom weaver in southern India taking the cloth he has produced to his co-operative for payment. It is difficult for handloom weavers to compete with those using powerlooms, yet machines will never be able to imitate the more intricate and varied weaves still produced on handlooms in some parts of the world.*

OPPOSITE: *Carved window frames in an old house in Kathmandu valley, Nepal. There is often a strong stylistic link between the architecture and crafts of a region, not only for cultural reasons but also because of considerations of climate and available materials.*

were regarded by Morris and his artistic friends as admirable alternatives to factory-made products. A similar attitude has become prevalent again today.

THE SITUATION TODAY

Since the 1960s in particular, momentous changes have taken place globally, affecting crafts production in a variety of ways. The great divide between rich and poor is greater than ever, with many "Third World" countries slipping ever further behind industrialized nations in living standards. This has been exacerbated by a number of factors, including the increasing national debt of such countries, falls in commodity prices and the enormous growth in population, which in turn has put pressure on land use. As a consequence, there is less food to support subsistence living, and many people have been forced to move to the cities in search of work. Even so, in many developing countries the vast majority of the population still live in rural areas, and large numbers of these people are reliant on the informal sector of employment – such as labouring on farms, running market stalls, and making and selling crafts.

The intensive cultivation of land advised in the 1960s as a short-term solution to the problems of feeding a growing population, and increased pressures on natural resources, including deforestation, have brought about considerable environmental changes. These have in many cases restricted access to raw materials used in traditional crafts: for instance, the world demand for hardwoods and rattans has led to a scarcity and to prices which local people cannot afford.

Media and communications have moved ahead at a fantastic pace in the last few decades. Popular culture now incorporates television and radio which show people in developing countries Western ways of life and a standard of living they never before thought possible. And, in the West, an increasing proportion of documentaries has been dedicated to traditional ways of life in the developing world. Microtechnology and air transport have brought new people and products into contact with each other, too. Computerized ordering systems may not have promoted the crafts themselves, but they have enabled them to reach a wider market, as orders are processed more quickly in response to fashion. Tourism has expanded and the cost of air travel has come down, so that more people are travelling greater distances; this has considerably opened up the market for "traditional" craft sold as souvenirs.

Inevitably the multiplication of craft production in response to these changes has led to new developments, and indeed some compromises in design and technique, in order for hand-made goods to compete in the marketplace. Some critics might say that these craft traditions are unrecoverable: but tradition is not static, and never has been. New crafts may sometimes undermine the old, but on the other hand, fresh traditions are being created. Since progress in the developing world is partly measured by the acquisition of manufactured items – plastic in place of clay or cane, for example – handicrafts are becoming less important to people, and may even be considered to symbolize a lack of progress. Sometimes the appreciation expressed by distant consumers can even help the producers to take greater pride in their cultural heritage.

TOP: *Painting the frame of a mirror; Lima, Peru.*

ABOVE: *Stitching an arpillera, Peru. Arpilleras were first made in Chile in the 1970s but are now made all over South America, with regional variations. There is a tendency to assume that craft traditions are static, but this has never been the case.*

TRADING FOR CHANGE

The traditional method of selling beyond the immediate community is through middlemen: if working as a family or individual, this leaves the craft producer vulnerable to exploitation. So, during the last 20 years, some producers have joined together to combat this exploitative situation – forming co-operatives or societies. There are a number of benefits to working collectively. In combining skills and sharing funds, they can reach out to a wider market by jointly promoting their products. Buying raw materials in bulk and jointly investing in storage facilities can also help, since it brings down the production costs. In working as a group, the producers may have greater negotiating power over fair wages and the prices at which goods are sold, and it can mean that individuals who have previously been exploited, can gain strength through solidarity. And when sharing work spaces and meeting regularly, not only are joint decisions made over the production and marketing of crafts, but initiatives to improve literacy, health and hygiene can also be realized. In many cases these developments have been supported by organizations concerned to tackle the roots of poverty. This handicraft production in organized groups has become integral to many development programmes round the world.

Development strategies of governments and non-government organizations (NGOs) have themselves developed and changed since the 1960s, when the emphasis was on financial aid and technological assistance to improve, in particular, agricultural production. Sustainable solutions had to be sought instead, and in the 1970s,

LEFT: *ADITHI is a self-help organization which is enabling women bit by bit to increase their confidence, education and economic independence. One way it does this is by marketing baskets. Oxfam Trading provided their first export order in 1991 after giving advice on costing and export procedures.*

RIGHT: *The basket this man is carrying holds a dowry gift that will help secure the marriage of his 11 year-old daughter; Bihar, India. Child marriages are still common here and poorer women have no say in how they live their lives or the size of their families.*

the phrase "Trade not Aid" was coined. The concept of putting people before profit was not new, but through the 1960s and 1970s many alternative trading organizations (ATOs) were established. They are alternative because they are concerned that producers should earn a fair return for their work and gain the means to tackle their poverty through their own efforts. As well as paying fair prices, ATOs pay an advance on an order, to cover at least the cost of materials. Along with providing market outlets for craft goods, ATOs can help producers with training in

product development and business skills, and so put them on a path to economic independence.

It is hoped that this celebration of craft skills and designs from the developing world will increase appreciation of the crafts themselves and create a greater understanding of the cultures in which they are produced. In placing the products in context, and by showing some of the people who have created them, perhaps the products will be viewed in a new light, and go some way towards giving the producers the recognition they deserve.

POTTERY

POTTERY RANGES FROM FUNCTIONAL WARES MADE TO SERVE THE ESSENTIALS OF
LIFE – WATER CARRIERS, COOKING POTS AND PROTECTIVE ROOFS FOR SHELTER – TO
THE DECORATIVE AND FESTIVE. IT COMES IN ALL SHAPES AND SIZES, FROM
ENORMOUS POTS FOR STORING RICE OR DYEING THREAD, TO THE MINIATURE
"SURPRISES" OF EL SALVADOR, TINY LIDDED OBJECTS WHICH OPEN TO REVEAL A
LITTLE SCENE. CLAY CAN BE TRANSFORMED INTO INGENIOUS PIECES FOR
ENTERTAINMENT, SUCH AS THE DUGI DRUM OF INDIA, A CLAY BOWL STRETCHED
WITH GOATSKIN, AND TERRACOTTA ANIMALS AND DOLLS ENJOYED AS TOYS BY
INDIAN AND BANGLADESHI CHILDREN.

ottery is perhaps the most universal of all crafts, produced by almost all societies past and present. There is something fundamental about this simple combination of earth, water and fire which plastic, for all its superb practical qualities, can never replace. Pottery is one of the first skills a civilization develops, and evidence of its practice is one of the longest surviving remnants after a society ceases to exist.

CLAY AND LANDSCAPE

Most pottery that is produced for local use and sale is made from local clays. The majority of these are so-called "secondary" or sedimentary, having been deposited by wind or water, or transported by glaciers which have shifted and then melted.

Generally, the secondary clays are the raw material of earthenware. They derive from iron-rich rocks and also contain "impurities", picked up during the course of deposition. The iron

ABOVE: *Mexican pottery made for the Day of the Dead.*

OPPOSITE: *Sasak girl carrying a waterpot, on Lombok in Indonesia; this burnished pot is for local use.*

OPPOSITE, BORDER: *Patterned bamboo weaving sticks, on which the decoration of incised Lombok pots is based.*

content causes the material to turn a characteristic shade of terracotta on contact with oxygen during the firing. However, in the raw state their colours range from soft browns through rich reds and greys to near-black. A physical boundary may form the line of distinction between communities producing very different pots; for example, in rainforest and upland regions of Peru, specific locations and types of mineral deposits have influenced local styles of painting with slips (watered-down clays).

In contrast with the deposited materials of earthenware, the finest white china clays or kaolins are examples of "primary" clays, because they are found still mixed with the crumbly granite rocks from which they derive. China clays have to be washed out of their parent rocks with high-pressure hoses and, after refining and drying, can be used as an ingredient in bone china and stoneware. These materials, which require firing at extremely high temperatures, are often transported some distance to the place of production (currently in the Philippines, ceramics are being manufactured from china clay

LEFT: *A pottery* dugi *drum; made and played by members of the Baul minstrel community, near Calcutta, West Bengal, India.*

BELOW: *A recently dug lump of clay is roughly modelled before being thrown on a wheel to create the bowl of a* dugi *drum.*

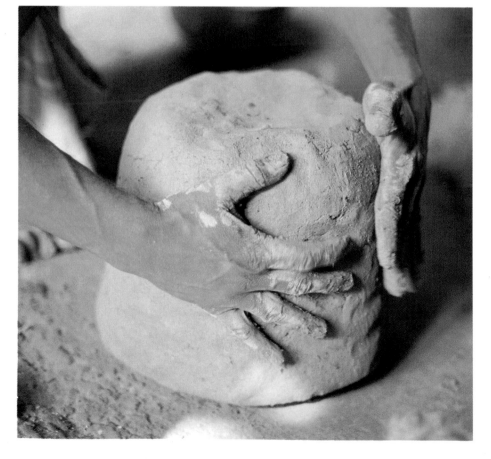

imported from England). Partly for these reasons china and stoneware are relatively expensive and are valued much more highly than the local earthenwares which form the majority of products and the focus of this chapter.

BUILDING BLOCKS

Pottery is simply baked earth (*terra cotta*), following a sequence of sifting, kneading, modelling, decorating and firing. Glazed wares often require a second firing. There are numerous variations on this theme, though certain principles are common to all pottery production.

The idea of making pottery may have come from coating baskets with clay for a degree of water retention. The development from coiling plant materials into baskets to making a pot seems quite logical, for in coiling the walls are constructed from the successive application of rolled ropes of clay. As the work progresses, the maker smoothes out the ridges on both the inner and outer surfaces.

Coiling and hand-building are probably the oldest known techniques of working with clay. In sub-Saharan Africa they were the only methods used until relatively recently, when an Indian potter introduced the stick wheel to Kenya in order to produce pottery for the growing Asian population there. Worldwide, throwing on the wheel is the most commonly used technique in hand-made pottery today.

The potter's wheel is like a rotating pedestal, which enables the potter to remain static as the wheel is turned, powered either by kicking a treadle with the foot, by spinning the wheel-head with a stick, or by electricity. But the neat, modern

stool-cum-wheel used by contemporary studio potters in the West today is an expensive investment, and requires controlled indoor conditions and a reliable source of electric power. In much of the developing world, human-power is still the norm.

ABOVE: *Use of the stick wheel is a male preserve in India; this is Neota village, Rajasthan, one of the main centres producing Jaipur blue ware.*

Other methods of making pottery include modelling with the hands, to produce sculptural pieces, and casting a shape with a mould. In the Jaipur blue ware of Rajasthan, some rounded details such as the rim of a jug are thrown on the stick wheel, but most shapes and sizes are formed

Coiling a pot in Penujak village, Lombok island (OPPOSITE); this method is used for large storage pots, but smaller cooking pots are hand-built by paddling (LEFT), using first the rough, incised end of the paddle (TOP RIGHT, shown with pebbles) for the approximate shape, and then refining with the smooth end, while a pebble is held behind the same spot. A smooth piece of igneous rock from the volcano in the centre of the island is then used to burnish the surface until shining. On some pots for the tourist or export market (TOP), patterns are incised by men (RIGHT), revealing the fragile, grainy texture of the local clay dug from nearby hills and carried down to the village in baskets. Pottery in the village is economically significant; women work from sunrise to sunset, averaging 6 hours a day in-between their other tasks.

by moulds. This technique of moulding is also used for making the little figures and objects in the *retablos* of Peru, although a few of these three-dimensional scenes in boxes are still hand-modelled.

As well as the available technology, the size and type of pot required can also influence the potter's method of working. On Lombok, a small island to the west of Bali in Indonesia, women potters in the village of Penujak use either a coiling or a paddling method to get the shape, according to the scale of the piece. The large pots with flat bases sit firmly on the ground whilst they are coiled into shape, and during subsequent use – storing the family's staple diet of rice. Smaller pots used principally for cooking can be manipulated on the maker's lap while she sits on the floor, legs stretched forward. As she works on her knee, with no flat surface, the pot has a rounded base, which will sit firmly in a crucible over the fire as flames lick around and evenly distribute the heat. Made from one lump of clay she beats it into shape, first by thumping and pinching with her hands, and then by slapping the outer surface with a wooden paddle whilst holding a stone against the inner wall at the same spot.

MIXING AND KNEADING

The technology used for creating the most traditional wares is nearly always determined by the character of the local materials. Some clay is like putty in the hand, pliable and plastic, presenting the potter with little danger of crumbling and tearing during the process of modelling. This kind is possible to use on a wheel, provided it is not so super-plastic as to lose its shape, or shrink excessively in drying; if this is the case it may be tempered with fine sand or a blend of minerals to turn it into a useful pottery material.

RIGHT: *Making Jaipur blue ware – the dough is formed in moulds, packed with burnt cow dung, and left to dry in the sun for a day or so before emptying out the dung. The rough surface of the pot can then be sanded to a smooth finish; Neota village, Rajasthan.*

BELOW: *An Indian woman sifting minerals to be mixed with water to form dough for the stonepaste Jaipur blue ware.*

This mutual dependence of method and medium means that if the wheel is introduced to a society which is accustomed to hand-building and coiling, the clay may require some modification. It can take years of experimentation to achieve the correct consistency, and force of tradition can be resistant to such change.

As local clays are usually coarse, containing "impurities", various methods of breaking them down to a powder have been devised. In Andean villages, lumps of clay may be seen outside the threshold of a house to be gradually worn down by the trampling of passing feet, and often the dry material is sifted or pounded. Agricultural and cooking implements may double up for this task – for example, a sieve normally used for grain, or a pestle and mortar.

Once reduced to finer particles, the clay is mixed with water and maybe additives such as minerals and sand. For example, the Jaipur blue ware comprises 90% quartz and a mixture in equal parts of: *sahji*, a volcanic-looking salt; Multani *mitti*, a sand of the region similar to Fuller's Earth, and also used by women for grooming their hair; gum arabic; green glass, produced in nearby Jaleshwar; and a finer transparent glass. These dry, grainy elements are mixed together and left to merge before water is added to create a clay of dough-like consistency.

Usually, the "dough" is left to stand for a while before it is kneaded; it is said that the clay will improve with maturity, and that the longer it is left, the more plastic the result. In many areas, a traditional method of kneading is with bare feet, having placed the wet clay on a goatskin. The foot method can also be seen in Bangladesh; but more often than not, the process is done by hand.

ABOVE: *Jaipur blue ware is painted with glazes of mixed borax powder, lead oxide and white crystalline copper sulphate, which will change from brown to characteristic blues and greens during firing, due to oxidation; the wares only undergo one firing, which is unusual. About 35 men and 5 women currently work in the pottery workshop at Neota; women are mostly involved in unskilled work – grinding materials for painting, and fetching water – while men are trained to prepare and use moulds and to paint.*

RIGHT: *Ninety percent of Jaipur blue ware production is exported. Most traditional are the blue and green wares, but more pinks are now appearing in the designs, as these are considered more appealing in the West.*

DECORATIVE MOTIFS
AND TECHNIQUES

The stage at which colour and texture are added to clay, and how this is done, varies tremendously from one region or area to another. One of the simplest and oldest methods of decoration – known through archaeological evidence – is to beat the clay with a cloth-covered paddle, leaving an imprint of the weave. But, for a more defined low-relief effect, motifs can be impressed into the clay with a carved wooden cylinder or roulette – a technique used in Bamessing, North West Cameroon where, with an action similar to rolling pastry (there are many analogies between pottery and cooking), patterns are transferred from the roulette to a strip of clay, which is then built into the sides of the pot.

Decoration can be added by simply pinching the clay between the fingers, to create a fluted edge around a rim, or by pressing a thumb print into the neck of a handle. Alternatively, when the clay is "leather hard", patterns can be incised by

ABOVE LEFT: *Carved wooden cylinders or roulettes used for low-relief decoration on a strip of clay; Bamessing, Cameroon.*

ABOVE: *The decorated strips are afterwards actually built into the sides of the pot. Such pots are being made in a centre in Bamessing established in the late 1960s to provide training and employment for rural people; a great proportion of the pots produced are being made for local use.*

stamping, or by etching with a twig. This breaks into the surface of the clay, often revealing a grainy texture beneath – an effect enhanced by polishing the clay beforehand.

This polishing process, which explores the flat shape of clay crystals, is known as burnishing and goes hand-in-hand with low-temperature firing. Burnishing follows the same well-known engineering principle as that of a highly-polished racing car; that is, because cracking tends to begin on the surface, if it is made super-smooth to minimize friction, the resilience of the product is considerably increased. Using the lowest technology, this is easily done with a smooth tool picked up from the local landscape; Sasak women use an obsidian rock from the volcanic range of central Lombok, but Shipibo women of Peru use the rib of a gourd on their pots. The result is a good-looking shine, and yet is quite different from glazing, which is mainly applied to make the clay more water-resistant and for colour decoration. And unlike glazing, which usually requires a second firing in a high-temperature kiln,

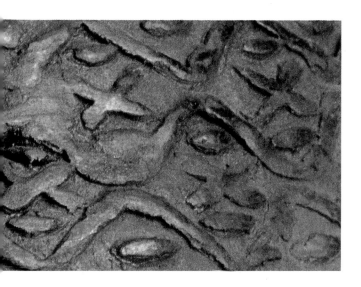

RIGHT: *Large pot painted with coloured slips, similar to those used in whistles and pottery portraits (see page 30) and also from the Ayacucho area of Peru. Slips are made from different clays of the Quinua area, which are ground down to a fine powder, then soaked in water for a few days; particles settle at the bottom, then water is poured off, and the top (finest) layer of sediment is used. Much of this pottery is traditionally made for wedding celebrations.*

burnishing does not entail expense and technical know-how.

In earthenware, for colour contrast, slip is used more frequently than glaze. Depending on its consistency, it can be laid into incised lines, or skimmed over the surface by means of a brush-stroke, or by dipping the pot into a bowl of the watered-down clay. Cooking pots and kettles tend not to be decorated, for they blacken with use over the fire. But pots for enjoyment are often highlighted with patterns. In Peru, pottery figurines of the Ayacucho region have two contrasting slips – one white, one dark brown – painted onto the red clay before firing. In these pieces, the decoration is used to explain the form and give humour to the facial expressions.

In other circumstances, patterns may be sourced from archaeological finds of the region, or from other decorated craft products. In Nicaragua, part of the ancient Aztec empire, motifs are being painted onto pots in a conscious revival of pre-Columbian practice. The incised decoration of certain Lombok pots, however, is based on

ABOVE: *Detail of bowl made by a co-operative in San Juan de Oriente, near Masaya, Nicaragua, from local, very fine, fragile clay. It is thrown on a wheel, then hand-painted with pre-Columbian-type designs.*

patterns carved into weaving sticks of split bamboo which are still in everyday use. The Sasaks' repertoire of motifs reflects a long and complex history of foreign trade in the Indonesian archipelago, for all sorts of subjects – from roses and floral scrolls to coats of arms and lions rampant – have been picked up and absorbed into the decorative crafts of the island.

LEFT: *Clamp firing in Penujak village, Lombok, Indonesia, a process for which the weather must be calm and dry. Pots are fired for just 25–35 minutes with any available combustible material. Some pots are then sprinkled with rice husks to deliberately blacken them; other pots char naturally over the cooking fire. Hundreds are put into the clamp.*

OPPOSITE: *Kiln at Neota village, India, for firing Jaipur blue ware. Firings take three days.*

tribution of heat leading eventually to cracking and breakages. It is during this delicate firing operation that the clay will be transformed into a more-or-less permanent form. This happens at about 600 degrees Centigrade, and the clamp or open hearth is just a little hotter than this.

The Lombok and Cameroon pots fired on this low-fired principle are ideal to use when cooking over an open flame, but they are not sufficiently durable to be transported long distances. For this reason a number of development projects have introduced kilns, which reach higher temperatures and ensure a more even distribution of heat, thus improving the strength of the product. In Penujak and Bamessing, for example, although the technique of building the pots remains unchanged, there are now two methods of firing. At Bamessing, those pots destined for local use are fired on an open hearth of burning grass; but the export wares are placed inside a brick kiln, constructed like a fat chimney with holes at the bottom for stoking and adding fuel – in this case, wood is used from a sustained tree-planting programme.

FIRING CLAMPS AND KILNS

The firing of pots on a clamp or open hearth is often a communal activity in which all the potters of the village or district, helped by their families, take part. In Lombok, in Indonesia, the event is rather like a bonfire party lasting a couple of hours. A bed of wood, rice straw, coconut husks and other available material is piled up. The pots – totalling hundreds, maybe – are laid on top, and more of the fuel is scattered over them. This can lead to uneven temperatures in the firing so, depending on how the wares are laid, irregular patches of colour will emerge – which is part of their attraction. The weather, too, plays its part. Word is passed round the community when the auspicious morning arrives; it must not rain, and the air must be still, as the faintest stir of breeze will whip up the flames, causing an uneven dis-

ABOVE: *Putting pots into a kiln accessed by the stoking hole in the bottom, in San Juan de Oriente, Nicaragua. The kiln is fuelled with wood, though in some production centres in Latin America kerosene is being used as a substitute for timber.*

FORM FOLLOWS CUSTOM

Shapes and sizes of pot follow cultural patterns, meeting the demands of everyday activities as basic as washing, eating and drinking. At first glance, the protrusions of a Cameroonian eating bowl look deceptively simple, and might once have been described as "primitive", but they are functionally and ergonomically perfect. The smaller knob helps the hand to get a grip on the bowl; the larger, open handle is designed to be hooked up on a wall. This is a common feature of

West African bowls, which are often decorated on the underside, their patterns being appreciated when not in use.

The black wares of Ranthambore in India correspond to the rituals and everyday customs determined by caste, religion and practical need, and in this respect resemble the pottery of many other Indian production centres. One vessel contains water; another is reserved for washing after defecating; yet more types of pots are for eating and cooking, and so on.

On the other hand, some pottery objects never have been intended for everyday use. Fun and festive, and occasionally macabre, they are not necessarily made to be lasting, but appear on special or ritualistic occasions. In India and Bangladesh, for example, there is a long Hindu tradition of making all kinds of fired clay figures for the great festivals of the year, and for other special occasions. There are three main categories: the gods and goddesses of the Hindu pantheon and their various incarnations; votive images of fertility symbols and other forms relating to local cults, some of them specific to certain villages; and animals of all descriptions – especially elephants – which were originally made as substitutes for sacrificial animals, and are now more often than not children's playthings. These figures are valued for as long as the celebrations last, then may be thrown in the river or left to weather and crumble. The clay is thus broken down and regenerated into new forms for future festivals and worship, as if the pots are as mortal as humans, and can be reincarnated.

Among the most colourful and dynamic objects of ritual are the painted pottery pieces sold at the roadside in the run up to Mexico's Day of the

ABOVE AND RIGHT: *Blackware from Ranthambore, patterned with impressions from small carved wooden stamps. The black colour is the result of the local soil which has a large silica content, and smoke from burning goat manure.*

ABOVE: *An elephant painted with black slip, made from local clay dug from the riverbanks of Bangladesh. Elephants are popular with the export market, and also locally as children's toys; they are made using the same modelling technique as votive clay figures of local Hindu deities.*

RIGHT: *Skeletons enjoying a feast: painted pottery made for the Day of the Dead (around All Souls and All Saints, 1 November). Decorations like this, and bowls full of the deceased's favourite food, are displayed on the offering table in Mexican homes.*

Dead festivities (around Hallowe'en and the next day, or All Souls and All Saints). Skulls, ghosts, and candelabra representing the cycle of life welcome the souls of ancestors. Pottery bowls and vessels are also specially made, and presented on the brightly decorated offering table, filled with the deceased's favourite food and drink.

Other ceramics made for festive occasions include the figurines originating from the Peruvian Andes, where there is an ancient history of portraiture in clay. Today, these represent amusing groups of villagers, some of them musicians with a hole made in the back, so that the hollow body can be played as a whistle. But as well as a long history of pot whistles, there is another tradition which the Ayacucho-type figures stem from: pouring portraits. With the hat left open at the crown, one of these is ideal for serving and drinking the local *chicha*. *Chicha* is an intoxicating liquor made from maize and widely consumed in South America; some Indians believe that heaven is a world where the souls of the dead are constantly replenished with the drink, without ever becoming drunk. One popular Peruvian tradition at festivities such as weddings is to give each musician in the band an amusing ceramic portrait of himself, pouring into it as much liquor as he can consume during the celebrations; in place of a financial reward the figurine is later taken home as a token of thanks. Special guests at the wedding may be recorded in a similar fashion, and each presented with her or his likeness in clay.

Also made for the preparation and consumption of *chicha* are the extraordinary anthropomorphic pots of the Shipibo Indians, who live in the Peruvian rainforest: rotund belly shapes, painted with linear patterns of thick, primary lines and finer secondary ones. The decoration is thought to be rooted in ancient symbolism, but its precise meaning has now been lost. Out of the maze of pattern emerges a face and ears, suggesting the presence of a *cucuman*, an ancient nature deity.

RIGHT: *Pots made by Shipibo Indian women on the shores of the river Ucayali in the east of Peru. Vessels like these are painted with brushes of human hair using slips of clays dug from the river bank; they are often used for* chicha, *the Latin American maize liquor.*

BELOW: *Peruvian musicians – the body of each figure is made on a mould and then assembled into a group by sticking them together with wet clay; a series of holes, cut into each hollow figure's back, means that it can be played as a whistle. The smaller band of musicians is made by the same technique.*

PATTERNS OF WORK

Exactly who produces the pottery, and when, differs from culture to culture, depending on whether the pottery is being made just for household use, or for sale as well. It is common in parts of Peru for a member of each household to devote one month of the dry season to the production of pottery which will see the family through the following year. This annual household task is necessary due to the built-in obsolescence factor of the low-fired pots. They are expected to break; and the broken shards are either ground down as grog, to add to the clay mixture for the next batch, or piled up on the roof of a thatched house, to fill a gap or to hold the old straw in place. Those pots whose bottoms have fallen out during firing can be adapted as chimney pots. (Other families make more than their domestic requirements, in order to sell – for example in the great pottery market of Cuzco.)

The division of labour between men and women follows apparently common patterns across the world, although similar customs and practices are not necessarily connected. On the whole, women are involved in making coiled pots (though in sub-Saharan Africa many male potters coil clay at a rate comparable with that achieved

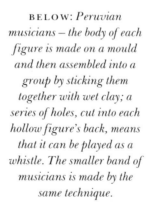

For every general rule there is at least one exception; but it is probably fair to say that either when a new technology is introduced, or when a craft becomes a more remunerative activity than in the past (sometimes both), it is almost always the men who adopt it first. In Lombok, for instance, where traditionally girls are taught to make pots by their mothers, the sons passively sit and watch and may help with looking after the baby or with other domestic jobs, but do not become involved in the craft. However, the situation has changed since the introduction of *sgraffito* decoration – an aspect of production which is relatively new, catering specially for the export and souvenir markets, and which has been taken up by men.

The shift from women's to men's production is not a recent phenomenon. It is thought that women may have been the very first potters, coiling and building clay bowls, cooking pots and storage jars as part of their everyday tasks. Their wares served specific functions within the household, and made a vital contribution to subsistence living. Nevertheless, once batch production on the potter's wheel and with moulds was established, professional male potters entered the scene. Similarly, in Kansongan village near Yogyagkarta in Java, freshly moulded horses, rams, and images of the celestial eagle Garuda, who carried the god Vishnu through the sky, can be seen lined up proudly outside virtually every house. The men who make them enjoy the status of artists and command high prices for their work, which is sold to middle-class Indonesians and tourists. However, their womenfolk receive very low returns on their skills invested in more humble items such as cooking pots, which sell for

by throwing on the wheel). The potter's wheel is traditionally a male preserve in India, for strict religious and social reasons. However, although the Indian technology has been introduced to East Africa by Asian men, it is Kenyan women who are now using the stick wheel.

ABOVE: *Throwing a pot using the stick wheel; Neota village, India.*

Young Javanese man filling a mould (TOP LEFT) for a pottery horse (ABOVE). Decoration for the mane and other details are modelled from small pieces of clay and added separately. The man (ABOVE RIGHT) who designed these figures is an artist of high repute on the island; here he adds finishing touches and inspects products from the workshop.

a pittance at the local market – though at least these can therefore be afforded by the local rural population.

One notable reversal of this situation can, however, be seen, as noted before: along Africa's east coast, the immigration of craftsmen from the Indian subcontinent has introduced new ways of making pots to the Kenyan people, resulting in Africans producing Italian-style wares for the local use of Asian people, and the women amongst them using a technology reserved for men in India.

The development of ceramic production has also had significant effects upon the social and economic status of its producers. The pots of Lombok, the island to the west of Bali in Indonesia, are traditionally made by poorer families in three pottery-producing villages; but the success arising from recent international interest in their work has benefited these communities, and they are now relatively better off than their neighbours who have no such craft to supplement the meagre agricultural living offered by the infertile central plain of the island.

SIGNS OF THE TIMES

As long as traditional methods of cooking last, the old techniques of making local pottery will probably continue, for they still have many cultural and functional advantages in their favour. The old-fashioned open firings can happen on communal land, are shared activities, and produce pots with good thermal shock resistance which are perfect for open-fire cooking.

However, adapting to a new source of energy for ceramic production can have radical social, environmental, and economic implications. Where wood is still the main fuel, overuse may threaten the local environment; to help prevent this, a carefully managed tree-planting programme has been established at the Bamessing project in Cameroon. Elsewhere – in some production centres in Latin America, for example – kerosene is now used in place of timber. Not only does this save the local plant population, but it also cuts down the time spent preparing the kiln; and the more efficiently powered electric or gas kilns enable producers to go ahead with firings irrespective of the weather, in which case pottery production ceases to be a seasonal activity. It also multiplies production and therefore, possibly, income. Nonetheless, if the Jaipur blue ware of Rajasthan were to be made with an electric kiln, as has been proposed, it would cease to be a "cottage industry" in the eyes of the Indian authorities, and would therefore be subject to higher excise duties, with the increased cost passed on to the consumer. This in turn could have a profound effect on the numbers of people employed in the industry.

RIGHT: *The wife of a potter sorting out bowls he has thrown on the wheel; Kakran village, Nayarhat district, Bangladesh.*

BELOW: *Fetching and carrying clay and pots is men's work, while the women make them at home; Lombok island, Indonesia*

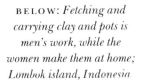

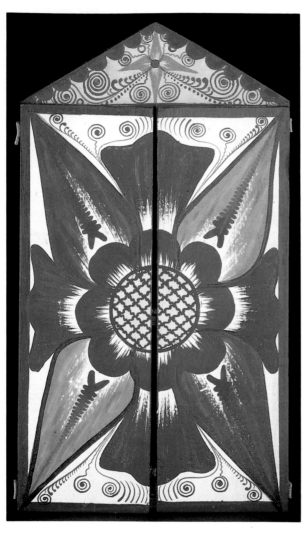

Retablo closed (LEFT) *and* opened (OPPOSITE) *to reveal Peruvian musicians above, and a hat shop below, made in a family workshop in the province of Ayacucho.* Retablos *come in all forms and sizes these days, with religious and secular subjects. This two-tiered effect commonly features a religious scene above – typically the Madonna, local patron saints, or a nativity scene – and secular subject-matter below.*

their mission to convert Andean peoples to the Catholic faith. Originally showing biblical scenes, images of the Madonna, or of patron saints, the subject has turned more secular, often representing aspects of everyday Andean life – frequently a shop – or folk customs like the scissor-dance, in which two men enact a lovers' duel. These themes have become increasingly popular as both tourism and the export market for crafts have expanded, as has the experimentation with new materials used for the boxes. Papier mâché is sometimes used in place of wood and today, fully aware of the fascination for all things miniature (and the convenience of their fitting into a tourist's suitcase), the *retablo* makers are even using eggshells, chewing-gum packets, or sections of hollow bamboo as the "boxes" of tomorrow.

These new ideas for the presentation of clay figures which are being experimented with in Peru are free from many technical constraints, since the figures are only dried, not fired. However, other groups of producers whose pots involve processes of burnishing, firing, and decoration with various slips, are changing their ways of working with the help of development programmes which advise on technical adaptation to meet the demands of the tourist and export markets; some outsiders' suggestions have been welcomed by these potters, whose need for income is greater than their attachment to tradition. Methods of working and styles of decoration are thus constantly adapting to new demands; but even so, many old craft techniques do nonetheless persist, for one factor which hardly changes is the nature of the local clay itself. Earthenware was one of the first crafts – after basketry – to be developed, and will probably be the last to disappear.

Hand-made pottery, despite its traditional roots, is constantly adapting to new demands, and always has done. The pottery *retablo*, a painted wooden box which opens up to reveal a three-dimensional scene modelled in clay or plaster, is said to be unique to Peru. In fact, the portable altars on which the genre is modelled date from centuries ago in Europe, and were brought to Peru by the conquering Spanish in the 16th century. These were used by travelling priests in

BASKETMAKING

BASKETMAKING IS ONE OF THE OLDEST AND SIMPLEST TECHNIQUES OF PRODUCTION – AND YET ONE THAT CAN PRODUCE THE MOST SOPHISTICATED AND VERSATILE RESULTS. USING CHEAP AND READILY AVAILABLE MATERIALS, FOR CENTURIES BASKETS AND RELATED OBJECTS WERE INDISPENSABLE TO MANY WAYS OF LIFE, AND YET WERE VALUED NEITHER FOR THEIR TECHNICAL NOR ARTISTIC QUALITIES. TODAY, THEY MAY BE HIGHLY COLLECTABLE, SATISFYING OUR VISUAL APPETITE FOR TEXTURE AND PATTERN AS WELL AS A FASCINATION FOR THREE-DIMENSIONAL FORM.

ABOVE: Werregué *basket, Colombia. Tightly coiled and stitched for carrying water,* werregué *baskets are no longer made for the Waunana people's own use (cheaper plastic is available), but fetch high prices as works of art.*

OPPOSITE:
Chellathangam and her two daughters coiling baskets in Manapad village, South India.

OPPOSITE, BORDER:
Detail of Thai bamboo bag.

P|alm fronds were the earliest fans and a whole leaf the first umbrella. A close observation of the natural growth of plants could have inspired the first baskets. Watching one being coiled, plaited, or looped into shape, it is easy to imagine how coiled clay pots, woven fabrics with geometric patterning, and knitting all grew out of this craft. However, although basketmaking was formative in the development of making useful and decorative containers, the processes of interlacing, twisting, or knotting plant fibres into pliable or rigid structures were not in the least confined to such items. In the tropical belt, where creepers climb up to the forest canopy and tree barks are extremely fibrous, leaf hats and barkcloth were probably the earliest forms of clothing, and the construction of these shared the simplest techniques as well as some of the materials of basketry.

The applications of basketry are endless: lidded baskets, hip-belts for body-tensioned looms, packaging for pots, panama hats, bamboo whisks, containers, belts, sieves, reels for winding thread, winnowing trays and hay nets, rattan chairs, cribs, hammocks and – on a much larger scale – the architecture of houses on stilts, woven bamboo wall panels and thatched roofs. It is even possible to travel by "basket": in an Indian coracle, or a reed boat across Lake Titicaca from Bolivia to Peru; upwards in an old-fashioned balloon; or, around 3000 BC in early dynastic Egypt, to the next world in a fine hamper-like coffin.

Some peoples have incorporated a language of basketry into their secular, religious and magical rituals. In Bangladesh, for instance, the *phuler shaji* is a flower basket used specifically for a *puja* or festival, when every home is filled with bouquets of colour in honour of a deceased person or for another special celebration. In some parts of the country a special basket symbolizes Lakshmi, the Hindu Goddess of Fortune, and is used in place of her image.

Though cut off from its roots and transformed, the spirit of the plant and a sense of growth almost lives on in the baskets made from it, and basketmaking requires sensitive respect on the part of the maker for the strengths and weaknesses of the plant.

PROCESS AND PURPOSE

The most contemporary basketry is extremely innovative, with new forms, functions and materials being explored. At the same time, some techniques and the products made from them, such as the Ethiopian grain sifter, have probably remained unchanged for centuries.

The main techniques are coiling, twining, stake-and-strand, plaiting, and looped and knot-

BELOW: *Splitting a* buri *leaf in the Pozorubbio area of Pangasinan, north of Manila, Philippines. The splitters produce several thousand strips per day, but the quality of raw materials is declining and as a result the suppliers must go further afield to get them.*

ted meshing. Coiling begins at a central point, and then spirals round and upwards as the core is wrapped or stitched into place. The core may be composed of a single strand or a bundle, depending on the local materials available – thicker cane will be used singly, but stems of short, thin grass will be bundled. The wrapping material can vary in colour and width: if narrow and soft, it is threaded through a needle or tool such as a bone awl, and is bound around one core and stitched

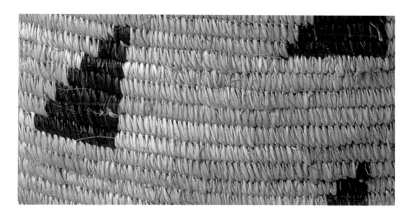

through the next; but if a rigid, pointed wrapping material such as cane is used, no such implement is required. Large baskets made from local grasses in Swaziland are sparsely bound by narrow plaited braids, leaving the different shades and textures of the grass core exposed; but in the palmleaf and *sikki* work of India, the wrapping completely hides the underlying core. Chequered and twill effects can be created by wrapping around one or more bands of the core. Alternatively, materials such as long strips of plaited braid are coiled and then stitched together with needle and twine. This technique is so simple and yet very versatile: it can be watertight like the *werregué* fibre baskets made by the

TOP LEFT: *Detail of bundle-coil technique on a log basket, Swaziland.*

TOP RIGHT: *Detail of a twined* tsero *winnowing basket, Zimbabwe, made from* ilala *palm fibre.*

ABOVE LEFT: *Detail of a Denju Nyanga reaping basket from Zimbabwe, showing the bundle-coil technique; made from* ilala *palm fibre.*

ABOVE RIGHT: *Detail of Ethiopian grain sifter.*

Waunanas in Chocó District, Colombia, or as finely stitched as the *igiseke* baskets of Rwanda.

In twining, a pair of (horizontal) wefts is twisted in the space between each (vertical) warp. The number of twists can vary, but often a half-twist is used. The *tsero* winnowing baskets of Zimbabwe, Kenyan *kiondo* baskets and large Ghanaian baskets, are some examples of this technique. The main characteristics are that the wefts are always pliable, and the warps are usually placed close together. However, a more open structure can also be created to serve other purposes, such as sifting. Sometimes twining is used to set the warps firmly in place before proceeding with another technique akin to weaving.

Stake-and-strand structure is just like plain woven cloth, but uses rigid materials such as bamboo, cane and twigs. The upright stakes are fixed into a basketry base, rather as the supports of a wattle fence are jammed into the earth, and the horizontal "weft" of twigs or stems is then

ABOVE: *Basket weaver using stake-and-strand technique to produce a lidded linen basket; Olongapo, Philippines.*

woven, one at a time, in and out. Scaled up, exactly the same technique can produce entire house walls; worked to lesser dimensions, with materials such as rattan and willow, stake-and-strand is equally practical for baskets and bird cages of the type produced in the Philippines.

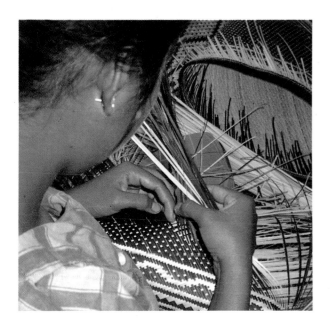

ABOVE: *Base of two-toned patterned basket from Kalimantan, Indonesia.*

LEFT: *Tiruray basket weaver finely plaiting; Mindanao, South Philippines. Exactly the same technique is used in Kalimantan, Indonesia, and the patterns are also closely related to those on some Thai baskets.*

RIGHT: *Detail of a plaited* chocolatillo *basket made by Waunana women in San Antonio de Togoromá, a tiny hamlet of just 22* tambos *(wooden houses) and 200 people, many hours' canoe ride deep into the Colombian jungle. The basket only takes a few hours to produce; it is quite flexible and is traditionally used for carrying fishing spears. Waunana women also make the* werregué *baskets (see page 37).*

babies' cots – and even to support gourd-like vegetables while they are still growing. The only support required during construction is a length of twine from which to hang bunches of threads.

Some baskets are constructed while the leaves and grasses are still green, and moisture and flexibility are retained – drying into a more rigid, permanent form later on. However, because most materials are dried and sunbleached after harvesting, soaking them in water helps to make them more manageable and supple during the making. This is especially true of cane and materials with a hard surface, which may well require other lengthy preparations such as scraping and splitting, and heating over a blow-torch.

Also akin to weaving, plaited strips intersect at right angles to one another, but they lie diagonally. For plaiting technique, three kinds of material can be used: a single fan-shaped leaf frond; long flat strips of, for example, bark or split bamboo (used singly if wider, or arranged close and parallel into a flat ribbon if thinner); and bundles of shorter-stemmed grasses. The mats and treasure baskets of Kalimantan are made of strips packed closely together, resembling smooth cloth to touch, but the springy Colombian fishing-spear carriers made of *chocolatillo* fibre are more openly spaced.

In addition, there is a whole family of knotted and linked meshes, which, unless made of a rigid material, can be extremely flexible. Some of the very finest net structures are the dilly bags of the Australian aborigines. Hammocks and *sikas* (the jute hanging baskets of Bangladesh) take on the shape of the object placed inside. *Sikas* are used locally for everything from bowls and bottles to

ABOVE: *A rattan, leaf and bamboo hat, made and worn for sun and rain protection by the Akha people, North West Thailand.*

LEFT: *Detail of inside view of Akha hat; the crown is plaited, then secured by a narrow band of twining, the rest woven to the brim in a balanced weave of four thin (warp) strips and one flat (weft).*

RIGHT: *Stripping rattan stems, using a concrete air-vent as a vice; Philippines.*

FIBRES FROM PLANTS

With a little ingenuity, it is possible to make at least something useful from any plant. Basketry could easily have begun as an *ad hoc* technique, appropriating whatever was at hand, in season, as necessary for survival.

Often simply called cane, the creepers most widely associated with basketmaking are the rattans. These are thorny climbing palms with rope-

like stems which use the forest hardwood trees as supports. Having grown to its maximum width, the rattan stem neither expands nor branches out but, clinging to the trees with curved "whips" at the ends of its leaves, grows upwards towards the light above the forest canopy, which it equals or exceeds in height – even up to 200 metres. In harvesting, the creepers are chopped through just above the forest floor and tugged away; the spines and leaves are immediately removed and the stems cut into manageable 3–5 metre lengths, then dried, graded by species or diameter, washed and bleached. Rattan is second only to timber in commercial importance as an exportable commodity from South East Asia's tropical rainforests, and the gathering and processing of it currently employs around half a million people in South and South East Asia. Most rattans are growing wild; even so, some species are increasingly rare, and therefore plantations have recently been established to guarantee a supply of good quality material, because as the destruction of tropical rainforests continues, this commodity is escalating in price.

This state of affairs has turned some old assumptions on their head, for throughout Asia in the past, rattan has usually been considered an ordinary, freely available resource for those people living in or bordering the forest. And although the majority of basketry is still made from local plants, some materials now have to be imported, due to the pressures of the export market for which the best quality rattans are reserved – especially for furniture. The repercussions are felt by the producers of typical local items such as the *mura* (stool), several versions of which are found all over India. For making this

ABOVE: *Detail of a Thai version of the* mura *(Indian cane stool), made from bamboo.*

ABOVE RIGHT: *Hiralal, with a* hukka *beside him, in Mayon village, Haryana state, India. He is making a* mura *(stool) of local* jhunda *grass bound with twine. A large stool like this takes a day to produce, and uses about 1 kilo of grass. Hiralal has made* muras *and winnowing baskets for the local market all his life, and supports his family from the craft.*

product, the better, thicker quality canes from the Andaman Islands are now extremely expensive and often in short supply, but the thinner untreated cane from Assam is more affordable, if not very strong.

Cane is also readily available in Southern Bangladesh, being indigenous to the marshy areas of Sylhet, Pabna, Barisal and Khulna. However, as the rest of the world witnessed in 1988, the country is prone to disastrous flooding, and one result is the loss of the raw material essential to the basketmaker's craft. Even in a kind year, good quality cane is quite expensive and therefore tends to be reserved for export products, in which case local bamboo is used instead for the home market.

The greatest number of the 850 identified species of bamboo, which belongs to the grass family, are indigenous to tropical and subtropical South and South East Asia, where they are prolific. In some areas they grow so densely that they are impenetrable by humans, smaller plants filling the spaces between the overgrowth of giant species. Bamboo's incredible strength (greater than some hardwoods) and speed of growth are legendary and have given rise to a rich symbolic language representing virility, long life, and regeneration. The shoots of some species are eaten;

leaves are used for thatching; canes for basketry; and the culms (stronger stems) for large-scale building. Each culm can be split into a fraction of its diameter and twisted into twine for binding the bamboo poles used for scaffolding or the frame of a building. Many Javanese houses are constructed in this way, then completed with woven bamboo walls about 2 metres high, strong enough to hold a weighty tile roof. The Sasaks of Lombok live in small thatched huts built of mud or bamboo on an earth floor, with a raised sleeping platform of woven split bamboo inside.

ABOVE: *Carrying a bundle of washed jute, wrapped with cloth; Bangladesh.*

LEFT: *Washing jute, with a recently harvested jute field behind; Bangladesh.*

OPPOSITE: *A knotted jute hammock in Kaurala village, India, where much* aari *work embroidery is produced.*

Jute (*Chorchorus* spp.) is an annual plant, growing 2.5–4 metres tall, requiring a monsoon climate. The fibres are extracted from the stem of the plant by retting (soaking in water) and are "soft" or bast because, compared with sisal for example, they do not contain much lignin. Bangladesh supplies 70% of the world's jute, and exports of it account for at least half of the country's income. There, the crop is currently managed by thousands of growers, each responsible for 1–2 hectares, though many producers of jute products such as *sikas* are landless and do not own their raw material. The initiative to cultivate jute for export dates from the British colonial period, when in the 1790s the curator at the botanical gardens in Calcutta and Madras, Sir William Boxbey, raised jute seeds and distributed them to growers. This enterprise led to the systematic cultivation of jute in Bengal to supply the UK with the raw material for rope, carpet backing, sacking and hessian. Dundee became the worldwide centre for processing the fibre.

Besides its value as a global commodity, jute has many local uses: the leaves are used as fertilizer; the sticks as fuel and for mud-covered walls; and a wide range of knotted hanging baskets and hammocks are made from its fibre. In the last few decades the bottom fell out of the world market for the raw material, largely because synthetics became the most popular carpet backing material. This is one reason why income generation through *sika*- and hammock-making has been so timely and appropriate, though this can make only the tiniest impact. Perhaps jute will make a comeback, because it is "greener" than the man-mades which have superseded it, being pollution-free and bio-degradable.

Relatively speaking, sisal is a so-called "hard" fibre, because of the stiffening effect of its lignin content. It comes from the succulent leaves of *Agave sisalana*, which originates in Central and South America and was introduced to East Africa in the late 19th century because of its suitability to hot, dry, coastal plain conditions, and where it is twined into Kenyan bags and colourfully wrapped in the coiled baskets of Swaziland. In Kenya, where the plants have been used to define special land boundaries, some producers collect the raw materials for free, though others have to purchase them. Sisal for the *kiondo* bags has to be peeled by drawing the agave leaves between the lethally

Savannah straw is used, split in two and then twisted by rolling between hand and thigh. In Swaziland, large coiled baskets are made from bundles of thin, round grass.

The raffia palm is grown in West Africa. Once processed, it is extremely soft and lustrous, and can be used for embroidering and weaving baskets, and even for cloth to wear. The fibre is stripped by hand or with a sharp knife from the upper epidermis of young leaves, and emerges transparent. It is then hung in bunches on a line in the sun to dry and turn its characteristic creamy-white shade, and afterwards is stripped into strands. The baskets of North West Province in Cameroon are constructed with the split central rib of a young frond of the palm, known as raffia bamboo, and then embroidered with bright, synthetically dyed raffia fibre. Particularly abundant throughout West Africa, the raffia palm serves many needs as well as being used as both a large- and small-scale construction material, it is also regularly tapped for a fresh supply of *mimbo*, white palm wine.

The soft, fibrous leaves and bark of the banana tree can be used as the material for rings to place on the head for carrying water pots, and for coiled baskets. But decoratively, banana fibre may be applied more selectively in dark patterns to contrast with lighter coloured papyrus and other stems, as in the baskets of Rwanda and Zimbabwe. An extremely good source for both food and practical materials, the longer fibres from the inner stem of the plant have been used for yarn, as for example in some ancient woven textiles of rural Japan. However, where bananas are grown as a cash crop, this takes precedence over basketmaking.

sharp blades of two panga knives; this is then twisted into twine by rolling several fibres together between hand and thigh – a very laborious preparation.

In addition, there are all kinds of local reeds and grasses used in basketry; few are exclusive to the African continent, but several varieties are widely used there. From one region or continent to another, as the botany changes with the landscape, there are corresponding differences in the durability, handle and fineness of its craft products. For the large Ghanaian twined baskets,

ABOVE: *Large twined basket of natural and dyed Savannah straw. Made in the Bolgatang district, Northern Ghana – basketmaking is the only regular income for these producers, who are mostly women. The baskets are made in many sizes for carrying market produce, for storage, or for collecting locusts.*

LEFT: *Applying dyed raffia decoration to a basket made from the split central rib of a young frond of raffia; Bali, Cameroon.*

RIGHT: *Box and Christmas streamers made of dyed palm leaf; these were just some ideas that resulted from a competition for members of the Edayansathu women's co-operative, South India. The price for the best new product is usually something practical like a bicycle*

BELOW: *Basket from Bali, Cameroon, decorated with raffia.*

In villages of Southern India, palm leaves grow abundantly and represent a lifeline to women whose husbands are either fishermen, or toddy-tappers (who climb up palm trees to tap the "toddy" or juice), or construction workers on sites away from home. Basketry is a new skill, learnt from necessity as the local fishing economy has collapsed. Palms are the one crop that can be relied upon in this drought-prone coastal area where there is only three months' agricultural work, and where the success of the harvest is entirely dependent on the monsoon.

ABOVE: *Plaited Chachi basket; the leaf is naturally darker on one side, so the maker alternates the faces to create a two-tone pattern. The Chachi Indians live in a pocket of rainforest, in North West Ecuador. Today the forest is shrinking and forcing change; some Chachis now make traditional baskets to sell. These are transported on home-made canoes to the nearest market town, more than 12 hours downstream.*

LEFT: *Cutting* rampira *for Chachi basket; Ecuador.*

RIGHT: *Zig-zag patterned baskets from Rwanda; the larger ones, traditionally called* inkangara, *are made by weaving the base and the lining structure with raffia bamboo, then criss-crossing an overlay of natural and dyed black stems of papyrus, stitching them in place with cotton thread. The smaller* igiseke *baskets are finely woven in a single layer over a wooden mould; these examples belong to a miniature set of five which slot into one another.*

COLOUR AND PATTERN

Expressions in pattern and colour are generally determined by the natural shades of the local plants, and the dyestuffs or tree resins available to tint them. The Chachi Indians in Ecuador use fan-shaped *rampira* leaves which, when cut into strips and arranged alternately face-up and face-down, create a two-tone effect in their baskets — the natural contrast in tone between each side of the leaf becomes apparent when the leaf dries. A more pronounced contrast of natural black and pale colours heightens the geometric grid patterns of the Htin basketry of Northern Thailand; the bamboo is interlaced with a black grass which has the great advantage of never fading.

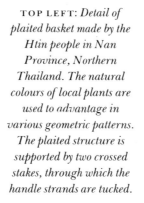

TOP LEFT: *Detail of plaited basket made by the Htin people in Nan Province, Northern Thailand. The natural colours of local plants are used to advantage in various geometric patterns. The plaited structure is supported by two crossed stakes, through which the handle strands are tucked.*

BELOW LEFT: *Detail of the base of a Htin basket.*

TOP RIGHT: *Detail of red and black plaited basket from Kalimantan, Indonesia; the colour is obtained from local plants, and is brushed onto one surface of the material.*

BELOW RIGHT: *Detail of base of red and black basket; Kalimantan.*

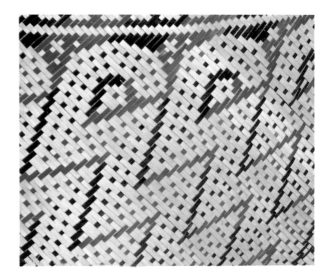

Some colours are brushed onto the surface, like the black and red resins used by the Dayak people of Kalimantan (formerly Borneo). In Bali, on the other hand, palm leaves are turned to mid- and deep-brown by burying them for a few days in earth, where the naturally rich minerals give the perfect combination of dye and mordant (the agent for chemically fixing the colour into the fibre). Half of the leaves are unearthed after a few days, and the other half are boiled up with ground-up teak leaves before a further 3–4 days' burial. The diverse natural sources of dye offer a rich palette for the basketmaker to play with, though particular combinations may be unique to an area. This is so in the heart of Colombia, where the distinctive yellow, brown and black of *werregué* coiled vessels is achieved with peat from the jungle floor and the juice of certain roots. The *kiondo* baskets of Kenya, with their subtle rainbow patterns, have traditionally been dyed with cowpea and pumpkin leaves for green, tea leaves and a local mineral for brown, loganberries for purple, and bougainvillaea flowers for lavender.

Some patterned baskets, such as the Rwandan *inkangara* and some of the Kalimantan plaited products, are double-layered – plain within and two- or three-tone without. Others are single-layered, but with patterns built up in shapes or wedges of colour, rather as in tapestry weaving. Some of these, such as the large lidded baskets of Cameroon, may be "embroidered" after the basket has been woven in patterns which do not

necessarily bear any relationship to the structure; however in plaiting the colours move in and out with the interlaced strips. Generally the coiling process allows the greatest degree of spontaneity, because it is easy to bring a new wrapping colour out of the bundle core to the surface, although the amount of detail and number of colours will depend on the fineness of the material.

BASKETMAKERS

The division of labour between men and women depends on the society to which the basketmakers belong; but, generally speaking, men tend to control the procuring of materials and the marketing of the finished product, while women put a great deal of their time into basketmaking – especially at the preparation stage. However, the women often receive unequal credit or payment for their time and skill. This is why much work is being done with the help of development agencies to enable women to upgrade their skills, including learning how to promote and market the baskets they make.

Throughout the world, women have to make things while going about their daily chores: in Bolivia women go around with a piece of knitting constantly in progress; in Lesotho they make baskets. Because craft production is often carried out in this way, it can be very difficult to cost the time involved. Sadly, for many basketmakers, the general public also have difficulty in appreciating

BELOW: *Men putting leather handles onto sisal baskets in Kariakar market, Naiwal, Kenya. There are several names for these sisal bags, according to where they are made, whether they are coloured, or of round or oval shape;* kiondo *is a traditional, round basket.*

precisely how much time has gone into their work. In Kenya, though the women make the sisal *kiondo* bags, they are generally not responsible for finishing them and taking them to the bigger markets. The men put on the leather handles and receive better remuneration for an input of minutes rather than hours. Kyu Ilumba, a member of Sofia Women's group in Machakos

district, described what goes into making baskets and the part the craft plays in the women's lives:

"Since my first sons are now married, I can put more hours in weaving because their wives can cook and attend to other farm activities . . . Me and the group is very ambitious. We have passed that, after every lady gets a water tank, we should start saving some money to buy our own maize mill grinder. This will earn the group some additional income . . ."

It takes most women one week to complete a *kiondo* bag, though Kyu Ilumba explained that as she grows older, she sleeps less so spends more hours on basketmaking and is thus able to produce about ten baskets per month. The finest *kiondo* bags are so strong and well made that it is difficult to imagine when they will wear out. They are superbly functional and beautiful to use, but because of their form and simple striped decoration, they will probably never be singled out as a gallery exhibit and command an "art" price. The growing competition from cheaper, less fine, but brightly coloured imitations made in the Philippines and in Latin America is not helping the future of the craft in Africa.

THERE TODAY, HERE TOMORROW

Of all imported products, surely the macramé hangings overflowing with spider plants have best come to epitomize the high street charity shop since the early 1970s. Now treated as a bit of a joke, the importance of their production and traditional use in the main country of origin,

ABOVE: *Backpack for carrying clothes, made from rattan and bamboo, and rainproofed with lacquer roughly applied over the surface; made by Karen men, Northern Thailand. Though totally utilitarian, this and many other kinds of unassuming baskets are now being collected in the West.*

Bangladesh, is largely ignored. There, the *sika* is an essential part of everyday life: it supports not pot plants, but coiled bamboo or ceramic bowls filled with grain and other possessions, hung from a bamboo pole which is part of the frame of the house. Many Bangladeshi houses cannot support shelves, for their walls of jute sticks are far too flimsy. Besides, suspending items away from both walls and floors helps to keep vermin and cockroaches away from the stores of grain, clothes, and any other valued possessions. The *sikas* are wonderfully practical for this reason, and also because they take on the shape of whatever is placed inside – small ones for bottles of oil, much larger ones for storing quilts during the summer months and as cribs for babies. Still in widespread use, some *sikas* are even being made from strips of plastic bag.

In the basketmaking world as a whole, however, many makers are no longer producing so much for their own use, since moulded plastic and woven nylon are much cheaper and easier to obtain. Increasingly it is the people of industrialized countries who value the natural colours and textures of traditional baskets, forming as they do a welcome contrast to the mass-produced factory goods in our homes. Some of the finest pieces – the *werregué* baskets made by the Waunanas of the Colombian rainforest, for instance – are now being treated as art, and are fetching deservedly high prices in Western galleries, reflecting the time and skill taken to make them. By a fine irony, much of today's cottage industry basket production is maintained by demand from the West, and the money earned from it is then used to purchase the precious machine-made items we have so long taken for granted.

CARVING

THE WORLD OF CARVING EMBRACES WOOD, STONE, GOURDS, MARBLE, AND
MANY OTHER HARD MATERIALS WHICH CAN BE GOUGED, CHISELLED, PECKED,
RUBBED, OR BURNED INTO SHAPE. THE CRAFT MAY HAVE ORIGINATED WITH
AN IDLE DOODLE, SCRATCHING ONE MATERIAL AGAINST ANOTHER, BUT HAS
SINCE DEVELOPED INTO MANY DISTINCT DECORATIVE TRADITIONS.
RANGING FROM ENGRAVED MINIATURE GOURDS TO MONUMENTAL
ARCHITECTURAL ACHIEVEMENTS SUCH AS BOROBUDUR IN JAVA, THE CRAFT OF
CARVING IS APPLIED TO A MULTIPLICITY OF FORMS AND FUNCTIONS.

Carving manifests itself in many forms. Hollow gourds are incised with patterns or stories, to make humble but decorative ladles and lidded containers in both Africa and Latin America; African carvings represent the humour and humdrum of modern life, as well as sculpted models of ancestor figures and narrative plaques; votive images of Hindu gods are still carved in parts of South and South East Asia; and highly coloured masks are chiselled with accentuated expressions for traditional Sri Lankan and Indonesian dance.

As with any craft, carving satisfies a fundamental human desire to make something beautiful; it also permits intangible ideas to be expressed in tangible form. The feel of a piece of carving can be as important as the object itself. The stone of Kisii in Kenya is sometimes referred to as soapstone (although, strictly speaking, it is not), because it feels soap-smooth to the touch. Votive images such as statues of the Shiva-lingam are touched as a token of respect, so that some of the spiritual power of the object can pass into the

ABOVE: *Stone sculpture of man with corn; Kisii Co-operative, Kenya.*

OPPOSITE: *A wood turner using a bow to turn the lathe and his feet to steady it; Saharanpur, western Uttar Pradesh, India.*

OPPOSITE, BORDER: *Indian carved woodblock used for textile printing.*

worshipper's fingers. In the case of sandalwood, a material used for images of popular Hindu gods and goddesses, the sensation of handling the materials is heightened by the scent of the wood.

Patterns, materials, and methods of work often suggest cross-cultural influence, and a design relationship between different forms and scales of work within the same culture. Carving is integral to architectural structures such as the wooden balconies and pillars found in Kashmir; Indian boxes of carved *sheesham* and inlaid marble are also linked to this Persian decorative tradition. The geometric patterning on a *bobok* from Sulawesi, Indonesia, similarly echoes details on the rice barns of the same region.

Not simply decorative, carving plays a significant symbolic and religious role in societies all over the world. The typical carved stone spirit house of Bali, usually perched on a pedestal, is a focus for daily offerings of carefully arranged leaves and flowers, a gesture of goodwill towards ancestral and other spirits.

Guardian images such as Indonesia's rice goddess Dewi Sri and India's elephant-headed Ganesh are produced in a range of sizes: larger

ones to appear at festivals, rising high above the crowd, or for incorporating in temple sculptures, and smaller versions for private devotion in the home. Carved protectors can also take the form of ancestors, and in Indonesia, although the strictest codes of Islam do not permit representations of the figure, because the religion was assimilated by peoples who already had strong animist beliefs, every Muslim house in Sumatra

ABOVE LEFT: Antiquing an image of Dewi Sri, the popular rice goddess, carved from semi-hard Pangalbwaya (crocodile) wood. Made by a family in Kemenuh village, Bali, Indonesia.

ABOVE RIGHT: Garuda, the celestial eagle; Bali.

or Java has a pair of splendidly dressed doll-like painted carvings, representing the man and woman of the household. And in some parts of Ghana coffins are carved into shapes symbolizing the deceased's occupation in this world, to protect his or her journey into the next.

Even so, it is interesting to note that despite the varied functions of carved forms, and the decorative versatility of chiselling, rubbing down, and

incising – whether onto sticks, seeds, or stones – some peoples do not express themselves through these skills. For example, although those tribal groups of Central Asia who have a carpet-weaving tradition have depended on wood for the beams and sticks of their looms, and for the poles of their goat-hair tents, they do not have a tradition of decorating the wood. Conceivably, where a culture and crafts are based on a nomadic lifestyle in an environment with few trees, it might seem superfluous to use a material and then cut part of it away, simply in the interests of ornament. Instead, imagination and observation of nature is poured into richly patterned saddle bags and carpets, made from the fleece of the livestock (and with which the plain wooden poles are hidden from view).

TOOLS AND MATERIALS

In carving, more than any other craft, the characteristics inherent in different materials determine the character of the carving that results, and what tools are used to bring the craft to life depends on the technology available. Slate is flaked; flint-like stone is chipped; igneous rock is pecked, ground and polished. As with stone, likewise with plants: different materials suggest various decorative possibilities. The hard-grained wood of Persia, for instance, which must be chiselled or chopped, gave rise to the fine geometric carving inlaid with ivory (closely related to inlaid metalwork, and with a similar appearance). A softer wood, however, especially if it is still green (which is much easier and quicker to handle than well-seasoned or hard wood) can be worked with a simple knife. The tough, smooth skin of a gourd

ABOVE: *Sandalwood Ganesh, carved in South India. Ganesh is the benevolent, elephant-headed cult figure featured in many embroidered* torans (*door friezes*); *he is a son of the god Siva, and being part-human, part-animal, represents the unity of opposites and the identity of God and man.*

RIGHT: *Carved pillar from Patan, Nepal – all older buildings in the Kathmandu valley feature carvings of this sort.*

LEFT: *A hunting scene pyro-engraved on a large calabash, from Cameroon, West Africa.*

yellowish in colour and close-grained; the darkish brown *nagagandha*, on the other hand, is used for its aromatic oil. Ideally, the sandalwood should be 100 years old before carving; traditionally it is felled long before that date, and left lying on the ground for white ants to consume the sap, leaving behind the aromatic heartwood. However, most carvers cannot in fact afford properly seasoned wood, which is becoming increasingly rare. Sapwood, which is softer and quicker to work, but which cracks and splits easily, is commonly used instead. A feature of such lesser-quality wood is its paler tone, but this is usually compensated for

can be decoratively scorched with a flame. And in Bali, gargoyle-like demonic and comic figures are carved into the trunks and limbs of trees. In such cases, it is not just the three-dimensional form imposed on the material which counts, but the natural characteristics of the wood itself which come into play.

Since the material is so crucial in determining the decorative possibilities, local botany and geology can influence the development of a style, though different producers create distinctive styles according to their religion and regional traditions and, naturally, personal inventiveness. To take one example, throughout the Indian subcontinent the climate, species of plant, and therefore availability of wood are extremely diverse. Thus ebony inlay is a specialism in Uttar Pradesh, and rosewood in Karnataka. Sandalwood carving, characterized by intricate detail reflecting the fine grain of the wood and the Indians' love of that style, is renowned in Mysore and Coorg.

There are different varieties of sandalwood: *srigandha*, the type mostly used in sculpture, is

ABOVE: *Polishing a sheesham box, with an inlaid brass design; Saharanpur, India.*

RIGHT: *Letter rack of sheesham wood, which lends itself well to this kind of* jali *(fretwork).*

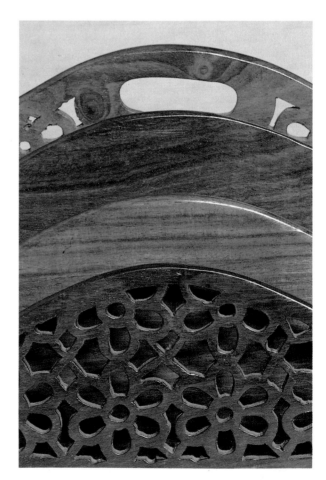

by one of the staining or polishing "tricks of the trade".

Sheesham and walnut were apparently worth migrating for, several centuries ago. The determination to continue practising a craft, based on a specific material and developed over many years, has caused some carvers to move or alter their patterns of work in order to survive. Persian craftsmen, in response to the large-scale felling of *jag* (*sheesham*) forests in their own territories, moved eastwards with the spread of Islam. They found comparable woods in the north of India, and thus the techniques of open fretwork so typi-

BELOW: *Carvers often work outside in the small yard of a house, also used as storage space, and home also to livestock; Saharanpur, India.*

cal of Near and Middle Eastern balconies and screens are found on many buildings and items of furniture in the Indian subcontinent. Some Persian carvers settled in Kashmir (which is still predominantly Muslim), where they began to carve walnut instead of *jag*. Others settled in Saharanpur in Western Uttar Pradesh, now the main timber market of India, and where their direct descendants are the *sheesham* carvers of today.

In preparing the stone or wood, unskilled workers are involved in quarrying or chopping before the block reaches the carver for rough-cutting. This initial shape is roughly chiselled out,

then the carver progresses gradually to finer tools to obtain the detail he requires. A smooth finish can be produced with a natural abrasive equivalent to sandpaper, such as shells, stones and, in Indonesia, rough leaves. Most carving is made from one solid piece; joinery involves another set of skills, such as mitring, pegging and turning on a lathe, and is mostly applied to the construction of buildings, furniture and other functional frames such as looms.

DECORATIVE THEMES

Many possibilities of decoration lie not only in the texture of the materials but in the way in which they are treated. The precise, linear quality of the inlay technique complements the hard, cold

ABOVE LEFT: *Detail of the front of a house in Srinagar, Kashmir, where methods of carving and painting wood are comparable with those of old Persian fretwork.*

ABOVE RIGHT: *Detail of a lid of an inlaid marble box: the same technique and similar motifs are found in the decoration of old Islamic architecture, including the Taj Mahal in Agra, Northern India, and buildings of the Near East. Carving of wood and stone is still a common trade in Agra today.*

marble used in Indian decorative boxes; much softer effects, however, are achieved by the low-relief carving of lighter-coloured, soft woods, as in the figurative plaques of Zaire.

In many cultures there is a close relationship between the decorative carving in architecture, and both two- and three-dimensional ornament in other media. The technique of marble inlay possibly originated, for example, from larger-scale architectural features. From written sources, we know that the idea of carving to decorate a doorway has ancient origins. The *Rig Veda* and the *Matsua Purana* of classical Indian literature recommend that all houses have door frames of carved wood to welcome guests. It is quite possible that the practices of painting around the entrance of the house and embroidering *torans*

(friezes) to hang there were inspired by a similar source. Links between architecture and objects are also strikingly evident in South Sulawesi, Indonesia, where the elaborate roofs and facades of traditional Toraja houses and rice barns are similar in style to the *bobok*, a type of lidded wooden container produced in the same area. The *bobok* is carved with a chisel and infilled with coloured earth to highlight the strong geometric patterns.

Some carved objects are specifically made to decorate another medium, though attractive in their own right. One example of this is the roulette, a carved wooden cylinder which is rolled over leather-hard clay, to impress a pattern into the surface of a pot. (An example of this from Cameroon is illustrated in the chapter on pottery, page 24.) Another instance is the carving of woodblocks for printing paper and textiles; the surface of a solid piece of wood is carved in relief, so that the desired pattern stands proud of the body of the block. The blockprinter uses this surface to pick up the print-paste and transfer the pattern.

Increasingly, since the 18th century in Europe and in 20th-century India, pins and strips of metal wire have been set into the face of the block, for printing narrow lines of pattern, and dots around spots. This development was partly in response to increased competition from the cheap machine-printed cottons produced in Europe where, by the early 20th century, block-printing had become almost prohibitively costly due to the time and labour involved. Another advantage of pinning the block is that it is a much quicker process than carving; it is also more durable, being less prone to warping.

RIGHT: *The* bobok, *a lidded wooden container, made in the Tana Toraja area of South Sulawesi, Indonesia; the design is chiselled out, and the background infilled with colours from local clays.*

ABOVE: *Indian woodblock for printing textiles; the craft of woodblock carving continues in some textile printing centres, especially around Jaipur, Rajasthan. Strips of metal are set into the wood block for fine dots and lines.*

ABOVE RIGHT: *Indian woodblock detail.*

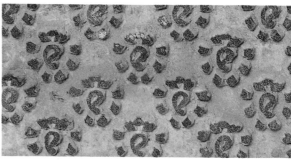

Currently, the art of printing by block is in decline, and with it, the tradition of carving, although some centres, particularly in Rajasthan, continue to produce excellent work and there is encouragement for the continuation of the art; new applications of the block-carver's craft are already being sought, and old blocks are even being incorporated decoratively into box lids.

LEFT: *Story gourd, Peru; this is a craft of the Sierra although the gourds themselves are grown in coastal areas. This example was made in a small, family-run workshop in Lima.*

Pyro-engraved gourd spoons (RIGHT) and calabash (BELOW LEFT), both decorated with a hot knife; Bali, Cameroon.

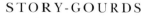

STORY-GOURDS

Gourds, once dried, are known as calabashes in West Africa and *mates* in Latin America. Cut across the top, they can be used for storing and pouring; halved lengthwise, they make ideal ladles. These humble implements have been used in place of and alongside pottery in some

ABOVE: *Figures carrying baskets and waterpots engraved on a calabash.*

OPPOSITE: *Engraving a gourd with a hot knife, in Bali, Cameroon; the ghetto-blaster at the carver's side is a sign of the times.*

societies; indeed, there is a strong regional resemblance between the shapes of some fired clay eating bowls and the local gourds. Engraved scenes as diverse as hunters in Cameroon, and everyday life in Peru, and simple geometric patterns, lines and spots, can be seen in the carved gourds of West Africa, Latin America, and other areas of the world where these hard-skinned marrow-like vegetables are put to both practical and decorative use.

Common to many gourd-carvers is the technique of pyro-engraving, literally meaning engraving with fire. In Cameroon, hot knives are used, scorching and incising the images simultaneously. In Peru, it is often the women who carve outline details with a sharp blade, and the men who highlight areas by blackening with a blow-torch or a piece of burning wood. Several effects are created by combining these techniques, either darkening the background, the lines, or highlighting the images in-between. Other variations include dyeing the gourd's surface, mostly with synthetic red or green, and then carving out images which appear white against the background colour.

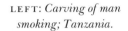

LEFT: *Carving of man smoking; Tanzania.*

RIGHT: *Sewing machine and motorbike; most carvers of this type of work from Malawi have small plots of land, but rely upon crafts to buy clothing, food and pay school fees. Images of modern daily life are increasingly included in the work of African carvers.*

ABOVE: *Carving from Vietnam, made from a highly scented cedarwood; carved by skilled craftsmen with a chisel and small knife in Hanoi. The old man with a stick represents longevity.*

SCULPTED FIGURES

Often believed to be imbued with spirit, or capable of enticing supernatural forces, carved images can have a powerful presence, whether realistically interpreted, or stylized and reduced to the most essential details. Vietnamese wood carvers produce figurines symbolizing, amongst other things, Happiness, Longevity and Wealth, which are presented as auspicious gifts. Carved figures can also reveal the carver's keen sense of

humour – this is evident in the African sculptures which represent people observed from life. Representations of, say, a man riding a motorbike or working at a sewing machine – a familiar sight in an African market – are 20th-century examples of such images. In time, these innovations of a new generation of individual artists may themselves be picked up and translated into new mass-produced forms. (Nevertheless, many craft producers today, with a basic livelihood and tourist market in mind, reproduce the same traditional patterns again and again.)

In the populous Kisii district of Kenya, where stone carving is the only commercialized craft and productive land is scarce, initiatives to produce new forms in Kisii stone have been encouraged by a local sculptor of some international repute. His book *Stories in Stone* relates the traditions of the Kisii stone carvers and he has been trying to help the carvers rediscover their own folklore, and express it in sculpture (see a man eating corn, page 57). At the same time, new technologies are being introduced and with them a fashion for simple functional ware. Kisii stone is extremely

LEFT: *Kisii stone fish plate; Kenya.*

BELOW: *Kisii stone mug and plate.*

smooth and, because of its softness, lends itself well to simple forms. After carving, the material is sanded down, washed, and can be coloured with a chemical wax; some, however, is left natural, allowing the characteristic pinkish tints of the stone to blush through.

CARVERS

Historically, the carver of wood or stone has enjoyed high status, possibly because of the responsibility he had to invoke images and spirits of powerful or beautiful creatures and things. In ancient India, for example, the master carver was known as the *sutradhar*, meaning one who holds the strings, or the key figure.

The question of who carves is not always determined by individual artistic talent, as a Westerner might expect. Many craftsmen work in family groups still, and the ability to carve might be explained as a talent passed from father to son (there are few women carvers around the world).

Occasionally, the process of carving a figure may fulfil a therapeutic need (such as a substitute child for bereaved parents), in which case the carver may be selected by a diviner who has consulted the gods; this practice occurs in Nigeria, among the Yoruba people. The producer's emotional relationship with the image, in such a case, is more significant than his creative talent – and obviously this is not the type of carving undertaken for financial reward.

However, throughout the developing world, an increasing number of people who are new to the craft are being apprenticed in co-operative workshops. Some producers take up the craft as a temporary means of earning money. In Central

LEFT: *Low-relief plaque, made by members of an association of individual artisans, working communally at a centre in Bukavu, Zaire. Members of the association can take part in literacy classes and a health scheme, and there are apprenticeships available for young men.*

administrative position than an individual carver to purchase supplies.

The serious problem of deforestation, however, has caused a tightening-up of legislation in an attempt to limit the supply of valuable raw material, especially hardwoods. Whilst such measures are in the interests of the environment, they pose a threat to the future of the carvers' livelihoods, since the legislative measures, although aimed particularly at larger-scale use of woods in the furniture and building trades, also affect production of smaller items on a more modest scale. Thus where carving of hardwoods has been a vital source of income, the producers may be forced to diversify and carve softer woods instead.

CARVING IN FUTURE

With regard to the sustenance of woods and forests, much depends on the volatile relationship between resources, employment and consumption. Some of the African timbers have become extremely scarce in recent years. In Malawi, ebony was used extensively for carving figures, but now a wood known locally as *nkolong'-onjo* is used instead. The future of many similar

Java, for instance, the carvers of dance masks who belong to a co-operative tend to work full-time while they remain unmarried; but later on, carving becomes subordinate to their main occupation, that of farming. Others are entirely dependent on carving. In Saharanpur, the principal timber market of India and a centre for *sheesham* carving, attempts to encourage the woodworkers, who belong to the minority Muslim community, to form co-operatives have been unsuccessful – leaving them open to exploitation as most are totally dependent on their craft as a means of earning an income.

Co-operatives can offer several advantages to producers who turn to carving out of need rather than vocation. As well as receiving practical support and training, and being able to develop as a group to seek outlets for their work, the members of a collective can be in a better financial and

ABOVE: *Smiling mask (topeng) made by the Kopinkra co-operative, Patuk village, Java, Indonesia.*

RIGHT: *The Kopinkra co-operative carve each block into two masks – one smiling, one not; a white base is applied before painting with bright paints.*

craft traditions around the world will inevitably change because the character of work cannot be replicated precisely in a substitute material. However, this situation may force fresh, creative ways of looking at the available resources, resulting in new traditions. The process of transition is already underway.

In the comparatively intricate sandalwood carvings of India, the difference between one figure and another lies not so much in the subject matter, but in the interpretation and skill of the carver. His skill is in regular demand, due to the number of Hindu festivals in the year instigating the purchase of new images. In Africa, on the

ABOVE: *Twisted spoons; made by the Makindu co-operative, Kenya, set up in the early 1980s for men of the Kamba tribe.*

BELOW: *Carved utensils for sale; Bangladesh.*

other hand, more novel items – such as carved and coloured walking sticks from Rwanda, spoons with twisted handles from Kenya, as well as numerous elephants, giraffes, and African heads – have a certain novelty value and "African-ness" which appeal to the tourist market. Whether the efforts to gain more income results in the development of new products or continuation of the "traditional" items and mementos, depends not only on access to export markets and the patterns of use within the local community, but also whether or not the products lose their relevance and identity once they are taken out of their original context.

THEATRE AND
MUSIC CRAFTS

AN INCREDIBLE AND DIVERSE RANGE OF CRAFTS ARE TO BE FOUND
IN THE PERFORMANCE ARTS. DANCE AND DRAMA CAN BE ENTERTAINING,
UPLIFTING, PROVOCATIVE, AND THERAPEUTIC; THE PROPS THAT SUPPORT
THEM ARE AS WIDE-RANGING – INSTRUMENTS, PUPPETS, MASKS, SETS AND
COSTUMES – DEMANDING SPECIALIZED SKILLS AND CREATIVITY OF THE
CRAFT MAKER.

T hroughout history, music and drama have played many different roles within society. Some forms of music are modified cries of hunting and fighting; for example, the *angklung* instrument, a rattle which is played in many parts of South East Asia but especially Java, was originally played to warriors to work them into a frenzied state of mind as they marched into battle. Drums and other instruments can also be used to induce states of trance, a necessary condition for people who are about to undergo a healing or initiation ceremony. In some societies, certain rituals act as a means of social control, and may utilize the incredible power of the mask to its full potential. The Lega people of Zaire, for instance, have ceremonies which formally acknowledge an individual's progression from one level of society to the next. Carved masks are included in Lega regalia, each type pertaining to a specific rank, so that the mask becomes a symbol of achievement.

Consideration of the media involved gives some idea of the diverse techniques employed in performance-related crafts. Wood is carved into slats for xylophones in Thailand and Cameroon,

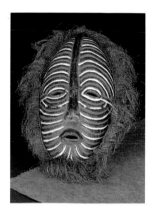

ABOVE: *Lega mask, Zaire, worn at masquerades.*

OPPOSITE: *T'Boli girl playing a* kubing, *similar to a Jew's harp; Mindanao island, Philippines. The resonant cavity is the mouth – the musician holds the* kubing *against the teeth, and adjusts the shape of the mouth whilst plucking the "tongue" cut into the middle of the instrument, creating an extraordinary range of tones and pitches.*

OPPOSITE, BORDER: *Detail of shadow puppets from southern Andhra Pradesh, India.*

and into funny and grotesque shapes for the masks of Sri Lanka and Java. Hollow tubes of wood and bamboo, cut to the required length, can produce precise changes of tone and pitch, resulting in the panpipes of Latin America and the *angklung*, of Indonesia. Clay is modelled into whistles in Chile, and hollowed into the bowls of kettle drums in India. All kinds of animal skins, from domesticated buffalo and goats to wild lizards and snakes of all descriptions, are stretched taut across drums throughout Africa, and beaten to a thin sheet for the shadow puppets of India and Indonesia.

WIND INSTRUMENTS

Wind instruments, including the whistles, panpipes and flutes of Latin America, make a noise when air strikes a sharp edge – either the mouth-hole or, more frequently, a rectangular opening at the end of a narrow duct. Most whistles, flutes and pipes are blown with the mouth, although in some countries, such as Indonesia, nose-flutes are played with the breath of the nostrils. Among the simplest wind instruments are the pot whistles of South America, some of which have only a mouth-piece opening, restricting them to just one

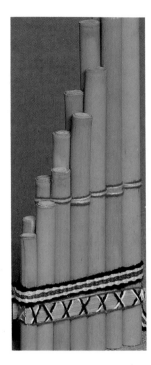

note. The head-shaped *ocarina* from Chile, however, has finger holes for playing scales.

In the past, panpipes, like whistles, have been made of clay, and on occasions have been buried alongside their owners. The breathy, haunting sounds of panpipes (*antaras* and *zamponas*) are instantly suggestive of Andean culture. These instruments are sometimes carved out of a single piece of wood, or alternatively constructed from a series of bamboo tubes. The length of tube determines the pitch, and the number of them, the range of notes. If the instrument has less than six tubes, it can be played in one hand (one finger per duct), leaving the other hand free to shake a rattle or strike a drum. The tubes of Andean pipes are often held together with colourful bands of woollen threads which can also be braided to form a neck strap. The *zampona*, like the intricately carved *tarka* flute of Bolivia, is held

vertically during play and is considered to be sexually symbolic; in Latin America at least, such instruments are only played by men.

PERCUSSION

Percussion instruments such as bells, rattles, thumb pianos, xylophones and Jew's harps, all made of naturally resonant materials, can be shaken, struck or plucked, and belong to the idiophone family. Whether wood, metal, or the skin of a gourd, each material produces its own sound. Made from all kinds of materials, rattles may have pellets trapped inside the vessel, like the beans in the giant bean pods of Queensland, Australia, or the rattle piece may be mounted externally – a knotted and beaded mesh, for example, loosely hung around a gourd. The principle of making sound by shaking pellets inside a rattle or bell is simple, but ingenious combinations of two or more different materials can give some interesting results. The cane basketry vessel used in the Cameroon maraccas, for example, modulates the hard tapping of pellets trapped behind the disc of calabash inserted just above the handle.

The *angklung*, a tuned frame rattle especially popular in West Java, is one of the instruments often used in the *gamelan* orchestral accompaniment to Indonesian puppet plays and masked dances. Traditionally, there would only be two or three large bamboo tubes loosely suspended in each frame; but a total of eight indicates that the instrument has been tuned to the Western octave scale. The instrument is not blown, struck, or plucked, but gently shaken, each tube in turn, causing vertical "flames" inside to rock and rattle

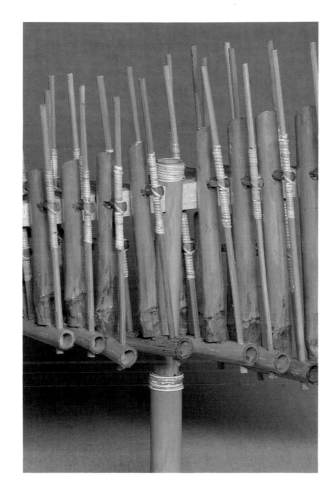

LEFT: *The* angklung *is traditionally made in West Java, Indonesia. It takes around 12 hours to make one* angklung *set.*

OPPOSITE: *Making an* angklung, *Java, Indonesia – Lili cutting tall bamboo for an* angklung (TOP LEFT); *Dais cutting bamboo to size for a particular note* (TOP MIDDLE); *Ibu Titin burning a hole through the top of one bamboo tube so that the frame can be slotted together* (TOP RIGHT); *and coating the* angklung *with varnish* (BELOW).

BELOW: *Thumb pianos, made from a hollowed gourd (Zimbabwe) and wooden box (Uganda).*

or flame); but there are many extra special effects besides, both visual and sonorous. Shells attached to the sound box, or little metal rings called brays threaded around the tongues, create vibrant additional tones and textures.

PLUCKING TUNES

Guitars, lyres and other stringed instruments (idiochords) are characterized by a sonorous body with one or more strings attached to it. The tube zither from Mindanao island in the Southern Philippines is plucked as an accompaniment to dancing, the melodies imitating the sounds of nature, especially rivers and the wind. Known by the T'Boli people as a *sludoy*, it is a hollow tube of bamboo with "strings" running down its length, which are actually thin strips of bamboo gouged out of the same piece; they are shaved slightly, and tensioned by slipping a small wedge underneath either end, so that the pitch can be adjusted. The *sludoy* is played particularly by T'Boli women; with the lower end resting against the

gently against them. The outcome is a mesmerizing, soft xylophonic sound, which is still used to accompany trance dances, especially of the "hobby horse" type.

Looking and sounding quite different from the other percussion instruments are the thumb pianos of sub-Saharan Africa, known by various names, but as *ndenge* in Cameroon. The player plucks the tongues of wood or metal which vibrate and cause the sound chamber to resonate. This can be an open gourd or an enclosed wooden box with a small hole at one end. Some are elaborately pyro-engraved (with a hot knife

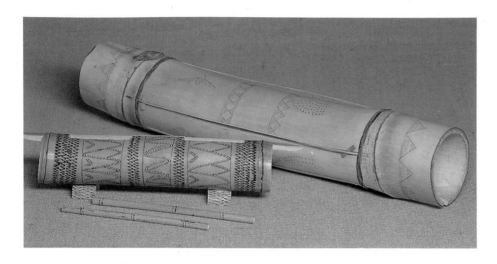

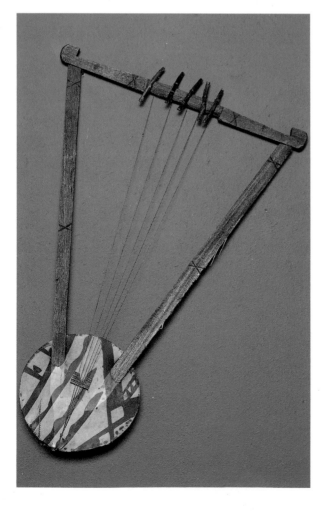

ABOVE: *A T'Boli bamboo* sludoy *from the Philippines, and a miniature "talking drum" from Bafut, Cameroon, with two tiny strikers.*

LEFT: *Ethiopian* krar *(lyre).*

body at waist-level, they hold the tube in both hands. Ingeniously simple instruments of bamboo such as this produce the indigenous sounds of remote South East Asian communities, although an instrument identical in design to the *sludoy* has also been found in Madagascar – perhaps an indication of ancient links of trade and culture.

Closer to European stringed instruments, however, is the *krar* of Ethiopia – a type of lyre, the strings of which lie in the same plane as the sound table and can be tuned to a fixed pitch. Legendary instruments of classical Mediterranean myths, lyres are still played in Ethiopia, Kenya, parts of the Sudan, Uganda and Zaire (and even Ireland). Though the sound box or bowl is usually made of wood, tortoise shells have also been used in the past. The sound table of hide or skin stretched tightly over the hollow chamber, also varies according to the materials available locally.

DRUM LANGUAGE

Take the strings and yoke away from the lyre, and you are virtually left with a drum, for the hide membrane tautly stretched over a bowl or frame is the key element in generating drum sounds – which is why this family of musical instruments are called membranophones. Drum makers are specialists; the job of chiselling out a solid block of wood to create just the right pitch is skilled work, and very exacting. Although the drum base is sometimes carved, the producer is not so concerned with form or decoration as with the audio effect of the cavity size, shape, and thickness of wood.

The various ways in which the membrane is tensioned not only control the pitch, but also contribute to the visual character of the instrument, and demand different skills of the maker. For example, there are many patterns of threading and criss-crossing the leather thongs around the outside of the barrel. Thigh-twisted goatskin strips, holding the cowhide membrane in place on a small drum from Malawi, have the same function as the hairy wool cords wrapped around the body of a much larger drum from the same region. Alternatively, the membrane can be fixed

BELOW: *Three drums: a carved drum with lioness faces from Cameroon, a dark wood and hide drum from Indonesia, and a twisted-thong hide drum from Rwanda.*

into place with bark fibre twine twisted around a series of knobs; these, and pegging devices tucked under tensioning cords, add incidental interest to the profile of the drum.

The materials used may be specific to an area. The base of the *ngoma* drum from Zimbabwe, for instance, is carved from the wood of the local lucky bean (*mutiti*) tree. And in Zimbabwe in the past, a membrane of zebra hide was considered to yield the finest quality sound. However, the most commonly used membranes today are goatskin and cowhide.

One of the most conversant of instruments, the drum is full of possible inflections. The beat can be reduced to a background rhythm, setting the momentum for other instruments to lead the tune, or it can speak alone. In either case, in many areas of the world the drum is of special significance. Like the gongs of Indonesia and the Far East, the talking drum was a very early means of communication, sending warning messages from one village to the next if an enemy was approaching. Because most African languages are tonal, the meaning being expressed partly through rhythm and pitch, it is possible to "talk" either by playing two different drums simultaneously, or by striking the same one in subtly different ways. Coupling the inflections with a

ABOVE: Drum-makers preparing hides to attach to drums; India.

OPPOSITE: Fixing hide membrane to the dugi *drum, made and played by members of the Baul minstrel community, near Calcutta, West Bengal, India.*

varied rhythm, the drum is, effectively, able to communicate almost as coherently as words, whether notifying the next village of a meeting at the chief's palace, or bidding the local congregation to church.

The large talking drums of Cameroon, which are played to gather the community together, are impressive, measuring around 90 cm long by 45 cm high, and weighing about 20–25 kg. Made of a hollowed-out trunk of wood with a long narrow slit down one side, they are still in daily use in rural areas of the country, where they are played to mark the hour of the day and at funerals and other ceremonial occasions.

The size of the drum not only controls the sound, but may be an indication of the way in

which it is played. The Ethiopian drums such as the *atamo* are quite small and portable, so that the drummer can dance and play simultaneously. In India, wandering Baul minstrels of Bengal – who for centuries have been entertaining at festivals with their allegorical love songs – wear two drums tied to the waist, the *dugi* and the *tabla*, kettle- and goblet-shaped and played with the left and right hands respectively.

ABOVE: *Peacock mask, Sri Lanka. Some Sri Lankan dances and the masks that go with them relate to Hindu myths.*

MASKS

Disguise and transformation are the objectives of masks, and possibly the richest repertoire of carved wooden ones belongs to Sri Lanka. There, the mask medium can invoke good and dispel evil spirits, as well as assist the narrative of a well-known folk tale in which familiar characters express the trials and tribulations of life.

LEFT: *Mask painter, Sri Lanka; the producers also perform the dances.*

RIGHT: *Dressing as Gurulu Raksha Natum for the dance; Sri Lanka.*

BELOW LEFT: *These are popular figures of the low country masquerade (kolam) dances; Olaboduwa, Sri Lanka. The drunken old man is Anabera Kolama.*

BELOW RIGHT: *Dancing with fire – a performance of the Demon Mahashona; special effects are intended to scare off evil spirits.*

durable, and easy to carve. After carving, the wood is primed with yellow and brightly painted (the old way of making them also involved drying out the wood by a fire, and rubbing down the grain first with a fish skin and then with rough-textured leaves). The decoration emphasizes bulging eyes, writhing cobras, and all kinds of accentuated human and bestial details.

The masks represent devils and demons, and also caricatures of figures: the masquerade-type dances incorporate commentaries on village life – during the colonial period these often ridiculed the Portuguese, Dutch and British officials, but today drunkards, old couples and the police are mercilessly and amusingly treated in the drama.

Sanni devil masked performances, on the other hand, derive from rituals to exorcise devils and to invoke blessings which will protect against illness. There are, for example, 18 *sanni* devil masks, each one representing a disease for which the devil is held responsible. To invoke blessings the dancers try to impress the gods by showing off their acrobatic skills, gyrating and somersaulting across the stage. The *raksha* demon dances incorporate fearful effects, known as *bayanaka rasa*, such as wafting torches and tossing resin powder around the stage to produce bright flames – an act deliberately designed to scare the audience. It is believed that by inducing such reactions, the effect of the evil eye (*eswaha*) will be crushed.

The Indonesian masked dance tradition (*wayang topeng*), strongest in Java and Bali, is closely allied to puppet plays. The dancers' angular movements, flamboyant costumes and painted wooden masks mimic in effect the small three-dimensional wooden puppets known as *wayang golek*, which have a long tradition of their own.

Masks, the theatrical effects accompanying them, and the time of performance, are often finely tuned to invoke specific responses in the audience, for each kind of dance or drama creates a different effect. The wearer of the mask, whether an initiate, a shaman, actor or dancer, adopts his disguise for very different reasons.

Since the element of disguise is crucial to the make-believe world of masked dance, in some cultures the producer and performer is one and the same person, thus holding the secrets of all aspects of dramatic creation. In Sri Lanka, the making of masks is confined to just a few families who have passed down their skills, and who participate in all aspects of creation, from carving and painting to performing.

A wide variety of materials are made into theatrical masks, including embroidered cloth, sheet metal, wood and papier mâché. Traditionally, Sri Lankan masks are made from wood of the *kaduru* tree (*Nux vomica*), which is light,

ABOVE: *Painted masks* (wayang topeng) *made by a co-operative in Patuk village, Central Java, Indonesia.*

PUPPETS

In many areas of India and Indonesia, both three-dimensional puppets of wood and papier mâché, and shadow ones of leather are made, although since each material demands a different craft skill, producers usually specialize in one type or another.

The job of making the elaborate three-dimensional *wayang golek* puppets of Java, which enact old stories from Arabia, was once confined

ABOVE: *Sujari chiselling slits in a mask for eyes. There are many young hardwood trees – teak, mahogany and ebony – growing in the area, but the carvers use the softer sengon. Young men work full-time on mask making, but farming takes precedence after they have married.*

to men; today, although the carving and painting is still done by men, women are involved in making the elaborate costumes and dressing the puppets. Styles of carving, painting and manipulating the *wayang golek* vary from one island to another. Those from Central Java are extremely stylized, representing human stereotypes, featuring Arjuna the perfect prince, the greedy Cakil, and so on (from the great epic poems of Indian history); but the Balinese puppets possess more individualistic human characteristics.

Traditionally, the Indonesian shadow puppets (*wayang kulit*, literally meaning play-leather) are made of thin hide supported by horn rods. The hide of young buffalo is most common, though goatskin is also used, and is specially prepared and intricately cut. After priming with white, each puppet is painted on both sides of the hide in rich colours, the best quality ones being highlighted with gold on top. The stamped lacy patterns, silhouettes and colours are all predetermined by symbolic coding; for instance, the faces of Vishnu and Krishna and their adherents are black, while Shiva's face is coated with gold, and others are pink. Representing characters of good and evil, princes and servants, devils, and buffooning clowns, a full set of these shadow characters numbers 200.

The shadow puppet tradition is predominantly based on the great Indian epic poems, the *Ramayana*, which features the popular hero Rama and the heroine and embodiment of womanhood Siva, and the *Mahabharata*, the war in which the Pandawa brothers battle with their cousins, the hundred Korawas. However, even before the arrival of Hinduism in Java around the 9th century, plays featuring cut-out leather shadows – portraits of deceased ancestors – were ceremonially performed in funeral rites and at other significant events.

Whilst the large cast of Hindu characters often stand for virtues – on which spectators over the centuries have modelled their own ideals of character and behaviour – and have retained much of their Indian identity, others such as the servant figures are of old Javanese origin. Interestingly, these shadows of servants and clowns act as devil's advocates, in that they throw in funny remarks

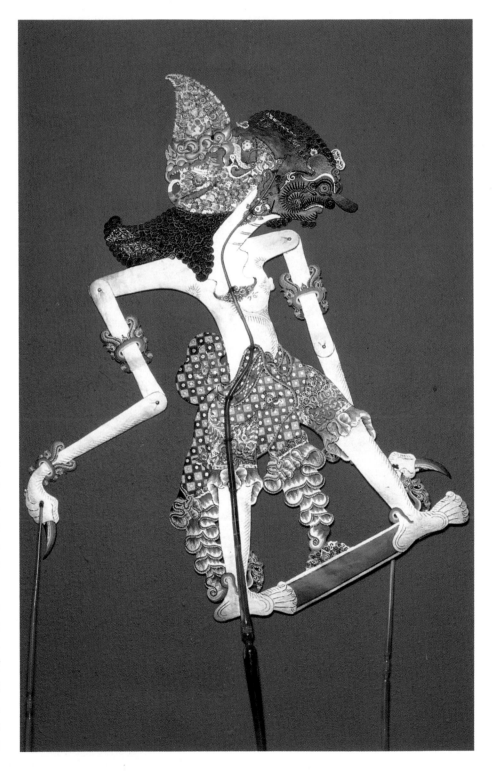

and the occasional sniping aside, both to relieve the dramatic lines of the protagonists and as a subtext of social comment. This kind of plot and exchange of character roles facilitates the double-edged nature of puppet performance: both entertainment, and a vehicle for disseminating information.

The *wayang kulit* puppets are colourful and fascinating in daylight; however, in night-time performance they are dark shadows on a canvas screen, being illuminated from behind by an oil lamp or, more often today, by electric light. Each side of the screen represents a different world, darkness and light, colourless ghosts and bright life, and the spectators during the night-long performance are free to observe the two. Behind, the masterly skill of manipulating the puppets can be viewed, as the *dalang*, or puppeteer, takes control of the total performance. He is not only a puppeteer, but the conductor of the *gamelan* orchestral accompaniment of gongs, drums, and *angklungs* when the epic reaches particularly emotional and dramatic moments, and he also narrates the story in an improvised fashion, shifting effortlessly from one character voice to another. The *dalang* probably had a priestly role when this dramatic art first began. Today he still observes preparatory rites before each performance; to please all gods and religions, his prayers are addressed to Allah and to local spirits, at the same time alluding to Hindu gods and the various aspects of Buddha.

The manipulative powers of the man who pulls the strings are also felt in India, where the puppet theatre has effectively performed all kinds of spiritual, medical and social functions. Although explicit political and sexual themes

ABOVE: *Shadow puppets of beaten hide; Andhra Pradesh, India.*

OPPOSITE: *Indonesian shadow puppet* (wayant kulit) *made by Usaha Bersama co-operative, Central Java, Indonesia; the co-op was founded by Pak Sukardi, a penatal (shadow puppet maker) who studied the craft with his grandmother.*

were strictly censored by the Mughals and later the British, the Indian authorities today use puppetry to advantage, in promoting government health initiatives. These performances can be an effective means of communication, cutting across the hundreds of regional dialects spoken in India.

THEATRE CRAFTS AND MUSIC-MAKING TODAY

It is clear that the origins of these crafts are often deeply rooted in ancient traditions arising from animist belief systems and from the great religions of the world, and that the roles of music and drama have been highly significant on a number of social, ceremonial and personal levels. However, in spite of their long histories, a large proportion of the puppets, masks and musical instruments being produced in the developing world today are aimed at the tourist and export markets, and many performances of "traditional" dance and drama are laid on for the benefit of foreigners.

There are many positive outcomes of this revived interest in indigenous theatrical forms, which has been growing over the last 20 years. It is providing employment for large numbers of producers and performers, and although at times the performance industry may appear extremely commercialized and superficial, underlying it is in fact a great deal of serious interest in the history of dance, music and drama. In many countries national theatre museums have been set up and, associated with them, workshops producing crafts which, if they were not preserved in such specialist centres, might be lost or forgotten forever.

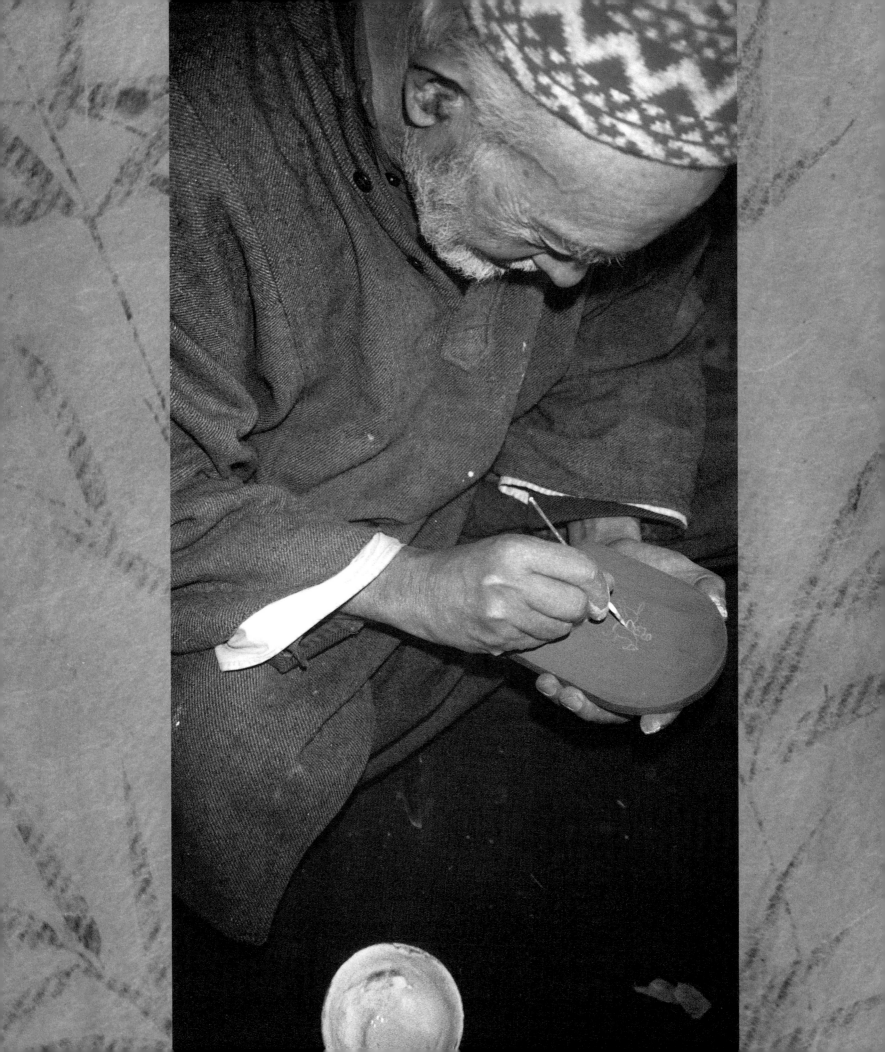

PAINTED AND PAPER PRODUCTS

HAND-MADE PAPER; PAINTED PAPIER MACHE; PAINTED PAPER KITES AND
UMBRELLAS; DECORATIVE PAINTING ON PARCHMENT, CLOTH OR PEEPAL LEAF;
BLOCKPRINTING IN INDIA AND NEPAL; SPRAY-PAINTING RECYCLED METAL IN
HAITI; DAUBING BARK WITH EARTH PIGMENTS IN AUSTRALIA; LACQUERWARE AS A
PARALLEL FORM OF SURFACE DECORATION – PAINT AND PAPER CAN BE PUT TO A
WIDE VARIETY OF COMMUNICATIVE, DEVOTIONAL, PRACTICAL AND PURELY
DECORATIVE USES, AND THE SOURCES OF PATTERN AND IMAGERY ARE AS RICH AND
DIVERSE AS THE MEANS OF CONVEYING THEM.

 ften patterns and styles of decoration are interchangeable across different media, the makers taking inspiration from memory and their immediate environment. Some images now adorning boxes from Peru are copied from the painted wooden beams from old Andean village houses. In Nepal, blockprinted hand-made papers are patterned with motifs reminiscent of pillar carvings.

Sometimes the decoration is traditional, the pattern dancing across a smooth surface and dominating the form, as in the lacquered wares of Thailand, Mexican painted gourds, or papier mâché boxes from Kashmir. In other instances, the painting is highly contemporary, as with the Colombian *chiva*, a miniature version of a real-life Colombian truck, its roof piled high with fruits and vegetables on their way to market, and the back filled with people and pigs and hens.

The use of paint and paper does not just apply to the decorative exterior of an object, but can form basic structures. Paper, though often thought of as fragile, can be extremely tough and

ABOVE: *Painted papier mâché lamp base; Kashmir, India.*

OPPOSITE: *Painting a papier mâché box; Srinagar, Kashmir.*

OPPOSITE, BORDER: *Detail of umbrella made of mulberry paper and bamboo, painted and lacquered; made near Chiang Mai, Northern Thailand.*

pliable, especially when it is hand-made; that is why it is so appropriate for umbrellas and kites which must withstand gusts of wind. It is applied to many more three-dimensional structures besides, including the bamboo-framed houses, cars, and aeroplanes burned in funeral ceremonies by the Chinese to ensure material comfort and prosperity for the deceased in their afterlife. Paper pulp need not be made into sheets, but can be mashed and modelled sculpturally, either freehand or around a mould.

The function of painting varies greatly from one culture to another. Some art is made for a specific occasion, whether to assist in a healing process, to celebrate a marriage, or simply to tell a story. Such items may have but a brief lifespan – a fairly alien concept in the West, where such items may be considered a lower form of art simply because they have no investment value. However, there are still many parts of the world where the adornment of body or house changes from one day to the next, according to the time of year, or the personal message to be conveyed.

Daily, in some Indian villages, women decorate the entrance to their homes, as a gesture of

LEFT: *South Indian woman decorating the entrance to her house; this is done on a daily basis, to welcome guests.*

welcome; the image must be renewed, even if traces of the previous day's work remain, or it will no longer be efficacious. These stylized patterns of pigment or coloured dust are seen as good omens. They include parrots, leaves, and other favourite motifs which appear in many guises in embroidery and other folk art forms. Such symbolic, but temporary, forms of decoration can also be seen in the art of body painting, applied in preparation for the rites of life. The Tiwi and other Australian Aborigines include this art in their ceremonies, and in South India brides'

hands and feet are painted with henna in intricate patterns – a craft known as *mendhi*. In all these cases, the act of creation or event that occasioned it may be more important than the decoration itself or its permanence.

BARK PAINTINGS

Painting is an essential aspect of ritual amongst the Aborigines of Australia, and is intimately connected with the people's knowledge of their land. Some of their work is portable, whereas

other paintings act as signposts in the landscape, permanently located on rocks or wooden structures. In the sub-tropical areas of Northern Australia, many paintings are applied to bark. They are stylistically defined by geographical areas and the subject matter is associated with the mythology of the Aborigine people who live there. Striking abstract images and stylized figures, applied in various earth pigments on bark, ranging from soft white to ochre and rust, may be highly significant. Sometimes the meaning depends on the visual effect of colour, sometimes on the

ABOVE: *Blockprinting handmade paper; Tulsi Meher Ashram, Nepal. The ashram provides a haven for abandoned women and their children; there is schooling available for the children, and women are trained in a variety of skills. This skilled blockprinter is teaching the women.*

location of Aboriginal land from which the pigment comes, and the event that took place there. Although apparently abstract to the uninitiated eye, even spots and hatched lines that have been reduced to pure pattern are more than just decoration, and can be clearly read. White spots, for example, may represent specks of sunlight reflected on rippling water, or honey bees swarming in a hive. Occasionally, special tools are developed to reproduce these effects. One, a small comb cut from wood for painting repeated dots, is unique to the Tiwi people.

The Tiwi live on Melville and Bathurst islands off the North Australian coast. Their culture developed in isolation from that of mainland Aborigines, and their mythology refers to the mainland as the "home of the spirit of the dead". Once Europeans established a mission station on Bathurst Island in 1911, European culture began to encroach on the lives of the Tiwi people. However, more recently, there has been support for the continuation of traditional arts of those islands.

These traditional craft objects being produced today reflect ritual items, in particular those featured in two Tiwi ceremonies. One, Kurlama, is an annual celebration of life; the other, Pukumani, involves elaborate rituals and taboos in honour of a dead relative, which are observed for between one and four months after death. For both these ceremonies, lengthy preparations involve the detailed painting of face and body. In the Pukumani ceremony, impressive carved funeral poles are erected around the grave, and their painted patterns are echoed in the detailed body painting and bark bags also prepared for the occasion. Large bark bags called *yimwalini* are used to present gifts to the dancers at the funeral; smaller versions of them, *tungas*, are now also made for sale. Making the "bark paper" for such baskets is quite arduous – the bark is soaked before being heated over a fire to make it pliable enough to be folded.

FROM BARK TO PAPER

Many tree barks are stripped and broken down to make paper. In Mexico today, there is just one centre remaining where bark paper, *papel amate*, is still made by the Otomi people of San Pablito in

ABOVE: *Tiwi decorated basket; Melville and Bathurst Islands, Australia. These painted bark-paper baskets, called* tungas, *are made from the bark of the stringybark tree, which is collected when the sap is flowing freely during the wet season.*

Puebla state. They used to use the bark of various fig trees locally referred to as *amate*, and also mulberry known as *moral* (mainly *Ficus tecolutensis* and *Morus celtidifolia* species for each respectively), although due to over-exploitation of these species, the fibre of *Trema micrantha* trees is now brought in from another Mexican state. The paper is made by separating the hard outer layer of bark and the more fibrous inner phloem. Fibres from the latter are boiled in water with some lime added, in order to separate and soften them. They are then arranged lengthwise and crosswise in a grid formation on top of a board, beaten with a special stone, and finally dried in the sun.

Where no indigenous tree bark suitable for making paper is locally available, a process similar to the making of *papel amate*, involving soaking, overlapping, and beating, may be followed using long strips of some other plant material. In Egypt, for instance, the sedge called *Cyperus papyrus*, conveniently growing on the banks of the Nile, is used.

Our word "paper" is derived from this papyrus; however, the standard process of making paper today is not to overlay strips, but to use a pulp. The Chinese are credited with the invention of paper-making, the history of the craft being based on a manuscript of the 2nd century AD, in which a technique of making paper from randomly arranged fibres is described. They realized the potential of the mulberry *Broussonetia papyrifera*, which is made into some of the most versatile and beautiful papers.

A wide range of hand-made papers is now being produced in countries such as Nepal, Thailand, Bangladesh, and the Philippines. Generally,

whatever is locally available is used. Thus in Nepal, for making *lokta* paper, bark fibres of the *Daphne cannabina* or *papyracea* species are used. The daphne shrub grows wild amongst the forest undergrowth at an altitude of 1200–1300 metres. The bark is removed in such a way as to sustain the growth of the plant, and is cut up in the mountains before being transported several days' trek away to the hill-farmers, who make paper during the winter when the workload in the fields is lighter. In Bangladesh, on the other hand, paper is made from waste jute and water hyacinths. The Shuktura project started experimenting with local materials in 1984, and

RIGHT: *Easing a newly-made sheet of paper off the sieve and onto a pile for drying; Shuktura Handmade Paper project, Bangladesh.*

BELOW: *Drying the paper on metal sheets in the sun. The Shuktura project was set up to generate income for women heads of household such as widows, abandoned women and unmarried women without fathers or brothers. Now around 70 women are employed.*

papermaking production began 5 years later. The paper is made from 90% waste jute and 10% water hyacinth, hemp or cotton; jute waste is soaked, boiled, then beaten into pulp before being washed and made into a slurry with extract of hibiscus.

Water weeds are also used in South India, where paper can include anything from tea leaves and rice straw to cotton and bagasse (the dry waste from sugar-making). Other hand-made papers are made from abaca fibre (from the wild banana tree *Musa textilis*) in the Philippines.

The use of materials such as water hyacinths and weeds for papermaking has additional environmental advantages, as the gathering of the weeds can stop a waterway from silting up.

Papermaking involves two stages. First, the fibres must be extracted from the plant and made into a pulp by softening and separating them in water, often with the addition of an alkaline substance such as lime or wood ash. They are then beaten so as to separate further. At the same time, this action roughs up the surfaces of the fibres, encouraging them to cling to one another.

The second stage is to convert the pulp into paper, by transferring the plant tissues to a tank of water; this suspension is called a slurry. The slurry is poured into or picked up by a rectangular sieve set in a wooden frame, which determines the size of the sheet. This frame is then shaken to ensure an even distribution of the fibres, and left to drain. The damp papers can then be interleaved (sometimes with a layer of felt between each sheet), and slightly pressed to squeeze out any excess moisture. Afterwards, the sheets are laid out to dry. One of the beauties of hand-made paper from countries such as Thailand is that the

OPPOSITE: *Nepalese* Lokta *(Daphne shrub) papermaking has recently been revitalized. The Daphne plant is cut down (*TOP LEFT*); the bark is stripped (*TOP MIDDLE*); and the soaked bark is then beaten into a pulp (*TOP RIGHT*). Slurry is then poured into the floating frame (*BELOW*) and, beyond, paper is left on the terraces to dry in the sun.*

RIGHT: *Mulberry paper flowers made by a women's co-operative, Maeteng Housewives Group, near Lampang, Northern Thailand. The paper is cut into petal shapes; each one is soaked in water, dabbed with cotton wool and then powder paint is applied to each tip, allowing the colour to bleed into the petal. Once dry, thin wires and glue give shape and hold the flower together. In 1988 the group received an award from the local provincial government for "outstanding" work.*

hot climate sun-dries the paper; its character is therefore quite different from that produced by the forced pressing and artificial drying processes of the paper industry.

The length of the fibres in hand-made paper also distinguishes it clearly from factory products and makes the paper much stronger and more supple. Different parts of the mulberry bark are used to create a rich range of products, from semi-transparent papers to the toughest and strongest ones for twisting into thread and weaving (a special technique in Japan), or for use in paper screens, umbrellas, and kites.

KITES AND UMBRELLAS

Spanning bamboo spokes or other frames, for centuries paper has been used for fans, kites and umbrellas. Mulberry paper is particularly appropriate, because of its long fibres and light weight, so many of these structures originate from the parts of Asia where the tree is most abundant, and where bamboo and lacquer are also conveniently indigenous.

Nowadays kites fly high at various festivals around the world, and their original significance and uses have largely been forgotten. The kite may in fact have begun as a military weapon, for carrying darts or measuring distances between targets. Legendary tales of China and Japan include daring heroes carried into the sky by these contraptions, the largest of which are still termed "man-carriers". Fighting kites are now used in a popular men's sport in countries like Pakistan and China: sharp pieces of porcelain or powdered glass are attached to the strong line of the kite, the aim being to cut through the opponent's line so that he loses his kite. Great skill is required for this.

Throughout the Malaysian archipelago, a wide range of fishing kites has also developed; in their prehistoric form, they take the shape of a large leaf supported by sticks. Regularly used by Asian fishermen today, with a baited hook attached to the end of the line, the kite is cast from the boat, travelling some distance from both the fisherman and the water's surface to avoid casting any shadow.

Some kite-flying is specific to the seasons. In India, where kites have been made and flown for hundreds of years, star-kites are flown at the

ABOVE: *Kite producer in Meket Noi village near Chiang Mai, Northern Thailand, constructing a bamboo frame for a kite. The business is family-run by two trained designers, employing around 11 people. The offcuts of paper from the kite-making are made into papier mâché boxes on the premises.*

RIGHT: *Peacock and snake kites from Northern Thailand, screen-printed onto mulberry paper and attached to a bamboo frame.*

beginning of spring, but Thai farmers have reason to fly theirs at monsoon time. They are flown to invoke the winds to blow, and carry on blowing; naturally, the rice growers wish the clouds to bring rain – but not to linger too long, lest the paddy fields be flooded to the point of ruin.

Kites have always been important and popular in the cultures which produce them. The recent revival is due to both tourism and the growing number of kite collectors and festivals in the

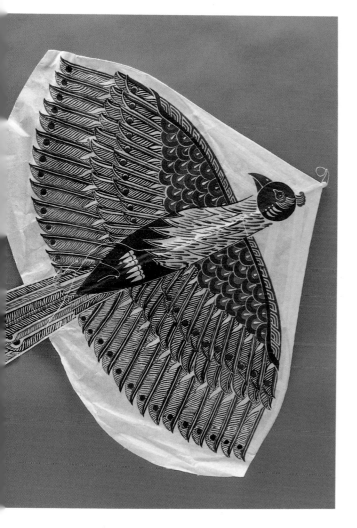

West. Decoration includes dragons and other auspicious creatures. The shapes of the kites can vary, but the proportions are crucial in performance. For a triangular kite to fly well, the tail of the kite should measure 10 times the length of the head. A large kite, on a good day, will fly around 60 metres high.

One of the biggest centres of kite-production is near Chiang Mai in Northern Thailand, where all the raw materials for the craft are locally available: the mulberry paper is made nearby, the

TOP RIGHT: *Screen-printing a kite with a dragon image, Chiang Mai, Northern Thailand.*

ABOVE RIGHT: *Fixing bamboo supports to a mulberry paper kite, Chiang Mai.*

bamboo for the frame is grown locally, and the kites are assembled in the same area. Today a large number of designs are screen-printed onto the paper, although in the past they would have been hand-painted.

Various villages in Northern Thailand specialize in making paper, kites, umbrellas, and lacquerware. Some of these craft centres have only recently been established, but Bosang village has been making umbrellas for at least two centuries. Thai umbrellas were originally made for temple

ceremonies and seasonal celebrations, in which they identified persons of rank. Some of them were of a magnificent scale, with the size and number of layers proportionate to the status of the user (the King of Siam's parasol had seven or nine layers). However, today the umbrella tradition has fossilized into a tourist attraction, whereby the producers and their skills are seen to be as much a part of the cultural experience as the products they make.

The tasks of umbrella-making are organized on assembly-line principles. One person will make the bamboo components of the frame; another will screen-print the design onto the paper or cloth shade; further along the village painters will do their work, applying symbols such as the crane bird and bamboo with loose Chinese-like brushstrokes. Some umbrellas are covered in cotton or rayon, purchased from

ABOVE: *A young boy painting an umbrella during his school holidays; Thailand.*

BELOW: *Paper umbrellas lying out to dry in the sun.*

OPPOSITE: *Glueing a paper umbrella onto a frame; Thailand.*

Bangkok. Others are made with *sa* paper from the bark of a year-old mulberry tree. Four layers of paper are used for most umbrellas, and each one in turn is painted with a mixture of persimmon juice and a secret ingredient to make a glue which waterproofs the umbrella. Finally, two layers of base paint mixed with kerosene are applied, followed by the designs painted in oils.

Skill is required in the making of these umbrellas, and the wages are based on a piece rate related to the intricacy of each producer's task. Generally, the whole community is engaged in some aspect or other of umbrella production, although many split their time between the craft and agricultural work. In common with weaving, production virtually comes to a halt in the wet season between May and October, when labour is needed in the paddy fields, and when paper and umbrellas cannot be sun-dried.

DECORATING WITH RESINS

The natural resins of various trees in Asia were probably first used for waterproofing and strengthening baskets and other objects made from plant materials, which are prone to moulding and infestation in humid climates. The technique of lacquerware began in China, but was perfected in Japan, and is applied to objects of all descriptions,

ABOVE: *The rak tree. Many people are allergic to this tree, the source of lacquer in Thailand, so only non-allergic producers can collect the resin for lacquerware.*

LEFT: *Sieving lacquer, Chiang Mai, Thailand.*

BELOW LEFT: *Jesus Parra with sons Xavier and Alejandro, decorating a plate in the* barniz *technique; Pasto, Colombia. Resin is heated in boiling water to make it elastic, with aniline dye added; it is then kneaded and stretched between two people's teeth to a thin membrane. For the* barniz *decoration, one layer at a time is stretched over the surface of the plate, stuck down with the heat and pressure of the hand, and cut to shape with a sharp knife; the next layer of a different colour is then applied and cut; and so on, until a multi-coloured pattern is built up.*

including spinning tops, chopsticks and trays, and bowls for presenting food.

Lacquer is a boiled sap, tapped from the trunk of the tree by cutting the bark with a downward slash, causing it to drip into a cup at the bottom. The very special finish of lacquerware depends on the meticulous preparation of the base material, and then the application of many layers. The procedure followed in Vietnam gives some idea of the work involved. The wood of the box or whatever is to be ornamented is first boiled, then rubbed down to a smooth finish. The design may then be painted on or applied in pieces of eggshell or mother-of-pearl, and the first of 12 layers of lacquer is applied. Each one must dry completely in a clean atmosphere, before the next application. One lacquer box therefore can take up to three weeks to complete.

Very fine, smooth bamboo baskets are also used as a base for lacquer in Vietnam, and as the foundation of lacquered dowry boxes made in the state of Orissa, India. Those women who produced such dowry boxes and bangles (*sankhas*) worn by brides, and other items such as pen holders and even figurines, which are decorated with thick layers of lacquer-like paint, became known as Sankharis about a century ago.

Although lacquerware tends to be equated with Oriental style, a number of natural resins are also indigenous to Latin America. One of these, *mopa mopa*, is only found in the Putumayo region of Colombia. The raw material comes from the seed pods of a tree, which are boiled for hours until they reach a consistency of chewing-gum. Originally it was used to waterproof earthenware pots, but it is now being used decoratively in *barniz*

work, applied to plates, boxes, and figurines; multi-coloured effects are achieved by dyeing the resin in different colours and overlaying them.

PAPIER MACHE

Papier mâché is literally mashed paper. The basic ingredients of the pulp may include items as diverse as offcuts of paper from a printing press

BELOW LEFT: *Bamboo dowry boxes made by Sankhari women, Orissa state, India.*

BELOW RIGHT: *Thai lacquer boxes (TOP), decorated with flower motifs; lacquered baskets from Vietnam, and Mexican painted gourd (BOTTOM).*

or from umbrella- and kite-making, cotton and hemp rags, and even cement bags. These are pounded to a paste, to which is added a binder, often starch-based, and maybe some kind of resin. The pulp is then modelled either around a mould or with the hands. When semi-dry the surface can be smoothed to a fine finish with an object such as a stone or piece of baked ceramic. Formation of a papier mâché shape requires

years of practice or intuitive understanding of the consistency of the material to get it absolutely smooth. However, there are some producer groups who are relatively new to the craft, and so the quality of craftsmanship – and with it, the character of the object – can be variable.

The next stage of designing and painting may involve a variety of colours and varnishes, synthetic or natural. In Kashmir, where papier mâché is believed to have been made since the 15th century, many of the designs relate to other crafts which originated in Persia and caught the imagination of the Mughal emperors who brought Persian craftsmen to Kashmir. The typical multicoloured floral patterns share some of the intricacy of the borders of a fine Kashmir woven shawl; others are more direct copies of hunting scenes and the flora and fauna featured in Mughal miniature paintings.

Today, Kashmiri papier mâché products include vases and lamp bases, trinket boxes and trays. However, in the past, the technique was

meticulously applied to one specific object: the penholder. This was a symbol of gentlemen, officials and scribes, who would go about with a penholder tucked under one arm. Gold details were included: either gold leaf was applied to the form first, and then the colours painted around it; or outlines of gold would be applied much later, before the final oil-varnishing. For the colour, in the past and very occasionally still, lengthy hand-grinding processes were the only methods available, using sulphur stone for yellow, white quartz for white, burnt cow dung for black, and pomegranate seeds for red. However today commercial water-based colours are more commonly used.

LOOKING TO THE PAST

Some painting styles are imported or derive from historic example; others are rooted in continuous folk traditions of decorating the house interior and objects contained within it. Skills are often passed down through many generations. Not all workshops, however, even family-run ones, have an uninterrupted tradition, and a conscious revival has come into being. Thus, in India there has been a renewed interest in some of the old schools of painting which were once exclusive to religious sects and locations of pilgrimage or favoured by the courts of the Rajput princes.

In Kishangarh, Rajasthan, paintings are produced on wood and on silk, taking inspiration from old paintings. One family has over 300 in their possession. Many of them depict scenes from the life of Krishna, the celebrated hero and incarnation of the Hindu god Vishnu. With his lovers, he appears in lyrical compositions set in

ABOVE: *Hand-painted and varnished papier mâché box from Kashmir, India. The producers of papier mâché are mostly Muslim craftsmen who have passed skills and designs down over generations.*

OPPOSITE LEFT: *Detail of paintwork on a papier mâché lamp base; Kashmir.*

OPPOSITE RIGHT: *Modelling the papier mâché around a wooden mould. After drying and polishing with a stone, the piece is hand-painted. Wherever the price allows, gold leaf is added over a layer of sugar and egg white. Finally, varnish is applied.*

RIGHT: *A painting on silk, featuring Krishna and one of his lovers in a composition harking back to 18th-century Mughal style; produced in Kishangarh, Rajasthan, by a family concern run by three brothers and an uncle with 17 employee painters who work on a piece-rate.*

romantic bowers and domed pavilions. The Kishangarh school flourished in the mid-18th century, under the mystic and poet Raja Sawant Singh, who adored the tales of Krishna. His chief artist was Nihal Chand, who was influenced by the Mughal court painting of the period, but developed a personal style which emphasized the curves and almond eyes of his figures. Something of that mood is captured in the Kishangarh paintings of today.

One co-operative in Peru, on the other hand, which is painting pictures on wood, belongs to a community whose history of decorative paintings in roofbeams remains well within living memory.

Today, a variety of subjects – including modern life – are portrayed. These painters remain anonymous, mostly because theirs is a decorative folk art, but often because the collective activity (sometimes more than one person will work on a piece at the same time) counts for more than a signature on one corner. There is much individual talent in Latin America, but in this case the expression of one brush is not considered so important as the solidarity of a group.

ABOVE: *Scratching through a painted surface to reveal the natural colour beneath, using a metal tool set in a quill; co-operative group in Olinala, Guerrero state, Mexico.*

RIGHT: *Detail of painted box; Olinala, Mexico.*

LEFT: *Aminta Flores de Manzilla painting a letter rack; Taller Madera de Jesus, La Palma, El Salvador.*

BELOW LEFT: *Painted box; La Palma. First introduced to the town by a local artist in the mid 1970s, the distinctive painting style is now widely practised and the mainstay of a thriving craft industry.*

LEFT: *Real-life* chiva
(local bus); Colombia.

BELOW: *Painted clay*
chivas, *from the Sanchez*
sisters' workshop, Pitalito,
Colombia. A modern craft
based on a long tradition of
miniature folk art.

NEW PROJECTS

Palm leaves were once used as the base for Indian miniature paintings. Today, the peepal leaf is subjected to arduous preparations and finely painted. This new craft began around 15 years ago, and is currently the focus of an income-generating project near Trivandrum in Kerala state, South West India. In the hillside village of Chellankode there are few opportunities for

LEFT: *Soaked peepal leaves; Chellankode village, Kerala, South India.*

BELOW LEFT: *Cleaning the flesh off a leaf after soaking.*

RIGHT: *Peepal leaf painters, Trppaadam, South India. Because there are not enough orders, a weekly quota has been introduced; the families involved are reliant therefore on small plots of land to provide the remainder of their income.*

BELOW: *Peepal leaves laid out to dry.*

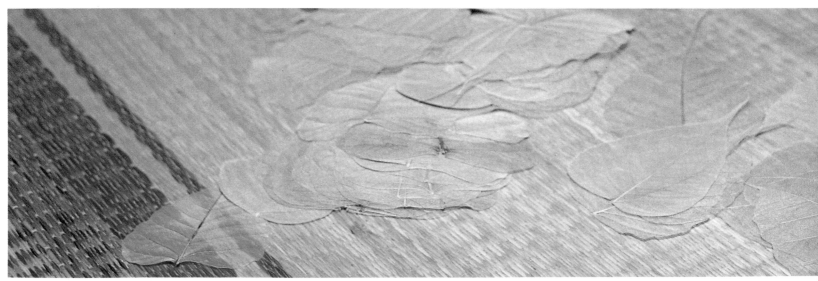

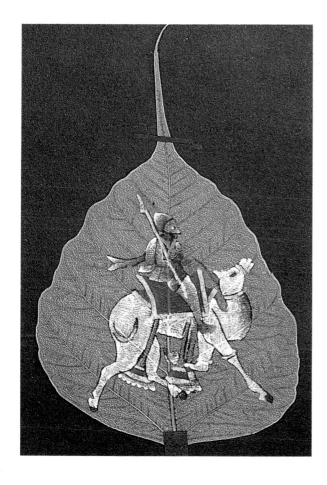

employment, but some families have found work processing the leaves of peepal trees.

Numerous leaves had been experimented with; but the peepals were found to produce the best skeletons. Thousands are picked from the trees while they are still green. Any with imperfections are discarded straight away; only a fifth will be suitable for painting in the end. The leaves are soaked in water for about one month, in order to break down the tissues. When ready, they are individually rinsed in a stream, carefully brushed clean, and left to dry in the sun – or inside the house so as not to blow away. By this stage, their delicate, diaphanous quality is apparent. The designs may be of people or nature; the outline is screen-printed onto the leaf, and then the colours are painted in. Since the market for the product is limited, the painters are given a quota.

In the painted peepal leaf project in Kerala state, and in the papermaking centres of Bangladesh and Nepal, it is foreign artists who have drawn up designs for the women painters and screen printers to work from. A thriving production line of greetings cards and gift-wrap is enjoying success, and bringing more much-needed work to local people. However, this depends on the commitment of artists and designers from the West, who are sympathetic to the technical and cultural values of the community in question but who also understand what images and types of product will sell. Too often, this kind of knowledge is what craftspeople lack, and it is difficult for them to understand why some products and not others have sold well on the international market. The challenge is to maintain a sense of tradition whilst enabling the producers to earn a living through their craft.

SPINNING AND WEAVING

THERE ARE VERY FEW PEOPLES IN THE WORLD WHOSE CULTURE HAS NOT
INCLUDED SPINNING AND WEAVING. WHEREVER THERE HAVE BEEN ANIMALS WITH
HAIR OR PLANTS YIELDING FIBRES OF SUFFICIENT LENGTH TO SPIN, WAYS AND
MEANS OF PRODUCING THREADS AND INTERLACING THEM HAVE DEVELOPED.
TEXTILES ARE ONE OF THE MOST EASILY TRANSPORTED GOODS; THROUGH THEIR
HISTORY, MOTIFS AND PATTERNS HAVE BEEN EXCHANGED BETWEEN CULTURES.
EVEN AMONGST ISOLATED COMMUNITIES, WOVEN AND KNITTED FABRICS HAVE
NOW SUPERSEDED OLDER TRADITIONAL MATERIALS.

Worldwide, the clothing and textile industry is, second to food, the largest employer of labour. Society's need for weaving and spinning, whether produced in professional workshops or at a domestic, subsistence level, is acknowledged in most languages of the globe: many familiar and poetic expressions were born out of specific clothmaking processes. Today, the majority of clothing is produced by machine in vast textile mills. Weaving cloth quickly has been the key to clothing a rapidly growing population and fostering – in the West, at least – an appetite for consuming fashion.

At first glance the world of spindles, wheels, looms, and shuttles may appear extremely complex. Certainly, it is magical to watch fine ikat of silk, cotton or abaca fibre being woven in South East Asia, or inlaid Dhaka cloth in the Koshi hills of Nepal. These extremely rich effects can be produced with the simplest technology of sticks and strings. Needless to say, all of the processes, from sorting a fleece to plying a fringe, are extremely time-consuming, making it hard for producers to compete with factory product.

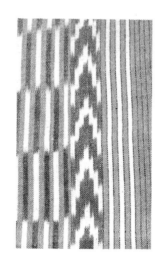

ABOVE: *Ikat detail; made by the Koyyalagudem co-operative in South India.*

OPPOSITE: *Spinning locally-grown cotton with a spindle, Sabu island, Indonesia; when the spindle is full, thread is rolled into a ball. Skeins of yarn are stiffened and strengthened before weaving by soaking in a starch-based size.*

OPPOSITE, BORDER: *Detail of Salasaca Indian tapestry, Ecuador.*

What is so special about hand-weaving is firstly that the tension in the cloth has a feel and character which the harder uniformity of machine-weaving cannot replicate. Secondly, because many cloths from the developing world are woven as panels (rather than continuous meterage), new thoughts and variations on the visual theme can be worked into each and every one – provided the weaver is given sufficient time and freedom to let this happen. The panels may correspond to the different dimensions of tribal Indian blankets, Indonesian shoulder cloths, a multiplicity of Nepalese hats, Guatemalan narrow ribbons and *huipils* (women's blouses), and so on. Within them, the decoration does not have to be distributed across the piece in relentless repeat; it is usually possible to pick up and leave off details – as, for example, an extra concentration of colour is introduced to the end borders of a man's *pattu* (shawl) from Rajasthan. The placement of the decoration corresponds to the traditional way in which a cloth is worn; the effect may be extremely rich, but in fact nothing is decorated unnecessarily. For instance, only one end of a sari or turban has a patterned border: the other is completely hidden by folds.

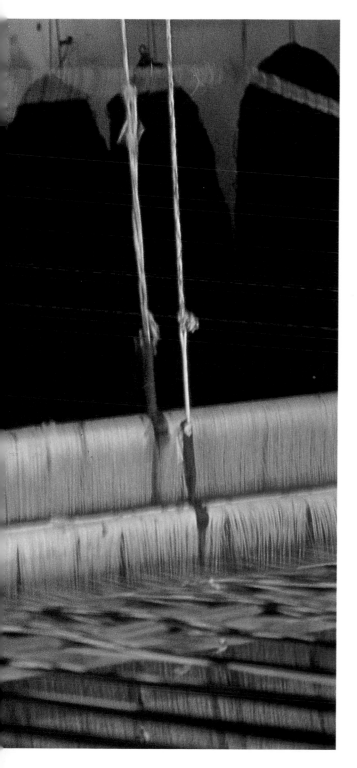

ANIMAL, VEGETABLE, OR SYNTHETIC

Geography and climate are the principal factors determining both quality and availability of fibres. Variously distributed within Latin America, Africa, and South and South East Asia can be found the plant fibres cotton, hemp, and abaca. Animal fibres include (moving from common to less common) sheep's and goat's wool, alpaca and various silks. Nowadays, most weavers worldwide have access to the synthetics developed in this century; acrylic and viscose rayon are most usual, but occasionally lurex or some other glittery yarn is woven into their work.

ABOVE: *Strap weaving in Totonicapan, Guatemala; the cotton cloth is used for belts and, in some villages of Guatemala, wound round into turban-like women's headdresses.*

LEFT: *Weaving cotton ikat; Koyyalagudem co-operative, Nalgonda district, Andhra Pradesh, South India.*

RIGHT: *An alpaca up in the clouds in the* altiplano, *Bolivia; its pale natural colours – white, grey and beige – command high prices because they are in great demand and not plentiful. In Bolivia this shortage has been partially compensated for by the import of alpaca from Peru.*

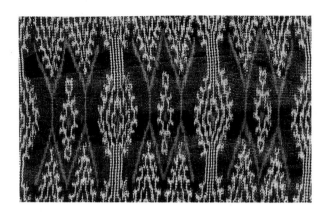

The cotton-growing belt lies between the latitudes 45 degrees North and 30 degrees South. Because cotton requires at least six months of sun, and a considerable amount of water, it can sap a country's resources disastrously if there is not sufficient rainfall. (This is the case in Uzbekistan, where water has been diverted to irrigate the cotton crop, and has reduced the Aral sea to a disastrous level, with terrible consequences in environmental terms.) The cotton plant is sometimes grown as the last crop in an exhaustive line of cultivation which may have begun with carefully balanced slash-and-burn (swidden) farming. Cotton is a mono-crop cash-based system, and as such, is encouraged by some governments and development agencies.

The cotton fibre is a seed-hair; each pod or boll is lined with thousands of them. Although there are more than 30 species of *Gossypium*, only four species worldwide are cultivated on a truly commercial scale as an extremely lucrative cash crop. However, pockets of indigenous cotton plants are grown here and there, including the natural brown cotton of South America, but generally these are only for local use in hand-spinning and weaving. Occasionally, cotton is now grown in

TOP LEFT: *T'Nalak cloth, Philippines.*

ABOVE: *A mother knitting with hand-spun alpaca yarn, near Juliaca, Peru; the craft is learnt at a very young age, and is mostly practised by women. A few men still knit in isolated areas such as Taquilla island on Lake Titicaca.*

place of hemp (*Cannabis sativa*), although the Akha people in Northern Thailand continue to grow hemp for their clothing.

Abaca, a "hard" plant fibre, is extracted from a wild banana tree, *Musa textilis*, indigenous to the Philippines and better known as Manila hemp. Extensively used in rope-making, and in some papermaking, it is woven on an extremely limited scale into the special T'Nalak warp ikat cloths by women of the T'Boli tribe.

Animal hairs vary enormously in quality from one part of the fleece to another, as well as according to the varied habitats of the different breeds, the diet of the herd, and the altitude of its natural habitat. Animals such as the rare mountain goats of the Himalayas and the alpaca and vicuña typical of the Andes, are coated with adequate thermal protection both for themselves and for the spinners who gather their yarn in the summer months to make winter clothing for their own families.

Silk caterpillars will only perform their marvellous cocoon-spinning act if the mulberry leaves mature at the appropriate time of year. What is marketed as "pure" silk is in fact the smooth, lustrous filament from the *Bombyx mori*, which was originally (and still is) cultivated in China. However, there are many species of silkmoth, and many of the regenerated sericulture projects involve the rearing of silkworms that produce what is often commercially termed "wild" silk. Tussah silk from Bihar state in India and Thai silk, for example, have a rougher feel than the "pure" Chinese variety – partly because of their comparatively high sericin (gum) content.

Ironically, whilst contemporary Western thought (reflecting current "green" issues to some extent) suggests that it is best to wear natural fibres and subdued hues of undyed, unbleached cotton and wool, to the peoples of those countries where hand-spinning and weaving are still routine, there is nothing more appealing than fluorescent synthetic fibres, cheaply available and ready made. Thus acrylic takes the place of wool in wonderful bands of inlaid pattern in hats worn by men in the Himalayan foothills, and the *huipils* and ponchos of Latin America.

TOP: *A silkworm (really, a moth caterpillar) munching a mulberry leaf.*

ABOVE: *Silk being reeled from cocoons.*

ABOVE RIGHT: *A straw weaver living in the valley of Gualaceo, near Cuenca, Ecuador, wearing a* macarra *(ikat shawl) woven by men, but using tie-dyed threads prepared by women.*

SOURCING MATERIALS

The production of cloth in developing countries can be influenced by social and economic factors of which the eventual wearer may be quite unaware. There is a delicate balance between the cultivation and supply of fibres, and the spinning and weaving processes. The craft producer is nearly always disadvantaged, having little purchasing power and certainly no influence over the price of the raw materials. On the Indian subcontinent, for instance, a clear demarcation of professional roles determined by traditional systems of caste or gender, or geographical location, play an important part. The Bania merchant caste of India, for example, controls the price of wool, resulting in a monopoly situation.

Factors beyond human control affect the balance too. In Rajasthan, severe drought caused half the sheep flocks to die of starvation in the years 1984–88. The price of wool rocketed due to the restricted local supply and consequent dependence on fleeces imported from New Zealand and Australia. Simultaneously, the weavers' earnings plummeted. But if the weather is kind, local wool for weaving *pattus* – the woollen shawls worn by Rajasthani men – and other items are available at more reasonable prices from the wool market at Bikaner.

Quotas and politically motivated trade embargoes can also affect whether or not developing

RIGHT: *Bowing cotton, in Sabu, Indonesia: the string is plucked to separate and fluff up the fibres; the same technique is also used in North East Thailand. On Sabu, traditionally the cotton seeds are separated from the fibres (seed hairs) by spreading them over the back of an empty tortoise shell and crushing them with a round stick.*

countries can export their textiles. The most formidable example of this in world terms is the Multi Fibre Arrangement (MFA) which is an "international agreement", signed in 1974, to restrict the exports of textiles and clothing from developing into developed countries. However, it is not just Western countries which impose quotas; the 1988 embargo on importing Indian goods into Nepal, for instance, caused a severe local shortage of materials for dyeing and weaving.

SPINNING A YARN

Spinning is deceptively simple, but it takes years to perfect the knack of drawing out fibres and twisting them together to make yarn. Once a single thread has been spun, it can then be plyed (usually twisted in the opposite direction to that of the spin) with one or more threads to make a thicker yarn. The length and lustre of a fibre and

LEFT: *Alpaca fleeces for sale at Juliaca market, Peru. Spinners and knitters often do not have spare money to buy new raw materials, so they sell their finished products at the market and immediately rush to buy another fleece as soon as they have cash in hand. Increasingly, knitwear producers are turning to factory-spun alpaca yarn (often mixed with another fibre) to keep the cost of raw materials down.*

There are many different degrees of sophistication and complexity in the spinning process. No tools are required for rolling fibres against the leg with the palm of a hand, a technique still used in parts of Africa and Asia. The spindle is still used in many rural areas, for example in Bolivia and Peru; this works on the spinning-top principle of a stick fixed with a whorl of wood or ceramic or stone, which gives weight and keeps the momentum of the spin going. The spindle can hang in mid-air – indispensable for use by shepherds or by nomadic peoples moving from place to place. Alternatively, the tip of the spindle may be steadied by a half-gourd or basket, or perhaps a nearby rock.

Likewise, the spinning wheel – or *charka* as it is known in India – follows several variations on a theme; whether made from a bicycle wheel or a wood or basketry structure, it can work equally well, and is adaptable to different fibres and techniques of winding and plying yarn. India is

the amount of twist put into the spin will determine whether a yarn is appropriate for making rope, knitting, embroidering, or weaving cloth. First, however, the fibres must be separated. Wool and cotton can be carded or combed; cotton is sometimes bowed to fluff up the fibres and simultaneously separate any residual dirt or seeds. "Bast" fibres – such as hemp (extracted from beneath the bark of certain cannabis plants) and jute – are broken down (retted) by soaking in water, then are dried and bleached in the sun, and raked or combed.

ABOVE: *Carding cotton in Kenya. The carder is a wooden bat embedded with wire pins; the raw fibre is placed between two carders, which are dragged across each other in opposite directions.*

ABOVE RIGHT: *Yai Chian in Sang Sa village, spinning cotton on a wheel; part of a village weavers' project in North East Thailand.*

113

thought to be the home of the spinning wheel, whence it came to Europe in the Middle Ages and was adapted from a cotton culture to spinning wool and linen. Being such a significant part of the country's heritage, hand-spinning and cloth production were perceived by Mahatma Gandhi as the key to India's independence from British rule. Lancashire's cotton mills were exporting tons of machine-spun, power-woven cloth (some of it made from fibre cultivated within the Indian subcontinent) at such a competitive price that it threatened India's own textile industry. *Khadi* (hand-spun, hand-woven cotton) was therefore worn by Gandhi as a symbolic gesture of independence, and he chose the city of Ahmedabad in Gujarat as the centre for India's "cottage industry" revival.

Cotton, being a relatively short fibre (quality is judged by length) must be spun to make yarn; however, some other very long fibres can just be separated and then spliced or knotted together into usable lengths. One such long fibre is the resilient abaca fibre used on Mindanao, an island in the Southern Philippines. The fibres are taken from plants at least 3 metres tall and about 18 months old. They are stripped by hand from the soft wet pulp of the abaca stalk, combed repeatedly to remove any impurities and to separate the individual fibres, and afterwards are bleached in the sun and knotted into long threads – used singly, not spun and plied.

THE PRINCIPLES OF WEAVING

Weaving is the interlacing of two sets of threads at right angles to one another. The warp, an arrangement of parallel threads tensioned

ABOVE: *Setting up a loom for weaving* lykhit *cloth in Sang Sa village, Thailand.*

ABOVE: *Weaving two-colour* lykhit *cloth in Sang Sa. The Village Weaver Handicraft project was formed by the Good Shepherd Sisters in 1982 to generate income amongst women; at the same time, the project has revitalized traditional weaving crafts of North East Thailand.*

between two sticks or beams, is the vertical, the weft the horizontal. Principally, there are three sequences in weaving: selecting and lifting certain warp threads to create a space (the shed); feeding weft, usually via a shuttle, into that space; then "beating" the weft into position to form a web of cloth. The sequence is repeated when another selection of warp threads is lifted. To make the simplest type of cloth (a tabby or taffeta), all the alternate (even) warps are lifted first, followed by the remaining (odd) threads.

It is possible to weave cloth with no fixed frame or loom. Plaited basketry, darning with a needle, and twisting threads into bobbin lace prove the point. However, if producing a cloth of some length in which the warp and weft threads are consistently at right angles to each other, and where the sequence of lifting warps is repeated again and again, it makes sense to regulate the successive actions by a frame and a mechanism for changing the shed – in other words, some kind of loom.

A loom may be free-standing, or it may be partially attached to a structural feature of a building, or even the weaver. The warp is held taut between the breast or cloth beam (nearest the weaver), around which the woven cloth is turned, and the warp beam (at the opposite end) which feeds the unwoven warp threads. Frame looms may be tensioned by any combination of stone weights, cords, cogs and pegs. But the body-tensioned loom, as the name implies, is controlled by the weaver herself: the breast beam is attached to a hip-belt, while the other end of the warp passes round a stick tied perhaps to a tree or verandah post. It is sometimes called a backstrap loom, a waist loom or a belt loom, and is used in

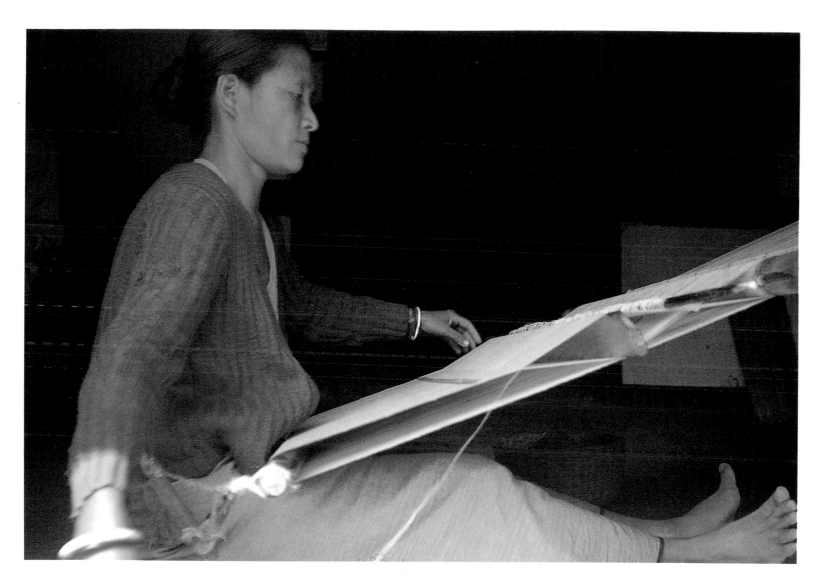

many parts of the developing world, almost exclusively by women.

Whether making a tapestry in a breezeblock shed in Peru, weaving in the space beneath a Thai house on stilts, or sitting in a pit in Rajasthan, a weaver follows the same basic procedure. The type of loom used will depend on the climate, the fibre and size of cloth, the weaver's lifestyle, and the materials available for building it.

ABOVE: *Uttarani, a weaver originally from Manipur in India, working on a body-tensioned loom in Sylhet district, Bangladesh. The width of cloth cannot be much wider than the hips, otherwise it would be impossible to maintain an even tension in the warp, or to insert the weft.*

PATTERNING ON THE LOOM

Sometimes the pattern of a cloth is determined before weaving, by arranging the threads in bands of colour for stripes and checks. Or, in the case of ikat, the warp or weft (or both, in the case of double-ikat) is meticulously bound with patterns to resist the dye. The coloured warps and wefts will create a bold or muted impression,

115

depending on how thick the threads are, how they are spaced, and whether the warp or the weft dominates the surface (i.e. whether the cloth is warp- or weft-faced, if not a balanced weave) in cloths such as twills.

In textiles such as brocading and tapestry, the weft is not continuous, because it does not reach across the whole width of the cloth. Techniques such as these, in which colour is fed from several little shuttles or spools, motif by motif, are extremely time-consuming. For example, with in-laid patterns of Nepalese Dhaka cloth, a 2-metre panel of a more complex design can take eight days to weave; because of the investment in time, this type of design will probably be worked in silk and sold through upmarket outlets. The patterns are in the weaver's head – about 100 of them – and variations on well-known themes are judged by eye, the fingers picking up the appropriate number of warps for each motif to insert the next pick of weft; and so the weaving progresses. Very rich, spontaneous effects can be created by using up small lengths of yarn left over from earlier weavings.

ABOVE: *Detail of Sagada cloth, Philippines, showing how vertical stripes are covered by strong weft patterns. The interest in this cloth generated by exports has led the weavers and local people to appreciate their traditional cloth once more, but they now favour working with acrylic-mix thread as it is more readily available than cotton; versions of the cloth are being made into backpacks for local schoolchildren.*

RIGHT: *Details of two cotton belts woven in Totonicapan, Guatemala; beneath them, a cotton* pattu *from Rajasthan, India.*

RIGHT: *Preparing warp before weaving cotton ikat, Sabu island, Indonesia.*

BELOW: *A group of ikat cloths from Sabu, showing patterns appropriate for women (floral/butterflies and men (geometric). Sabu island is one of the more isolated in Indonesia, and traditional techniques continue.*

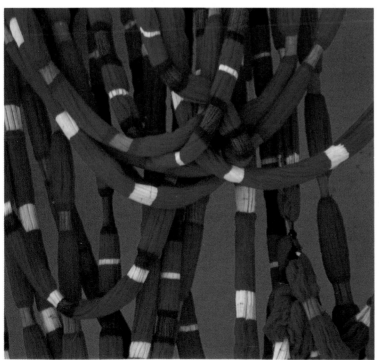

Indonesia has a fine tradition of ikat weaving, each island in the archipelago having distinctive characteristics to their work. Even within the space of a small island like Sabu, about 14 hours' ferry ride off the coast of West Timor, there are enormous variations in design, although the technique, materials, and many of the colours are identical to those of Sumba, Flores, Sumatra, Timor, and other islands of the archipelago.

The subtleties of language expressed through the patterns and motifs are really only understood by the Sabu people themselves. The distinction between men's and women's appearance is not just to do with the cut and method of wrapping garments, but the motifs woven into their ikat cloth. Men's patterns are predominantly geometric, featuring zig-zags, stars, and diamonds, as well as the very stylized Sabu flower motif (*boda*). Bands of these patterns are outlined by narrow two-colour stripes. The same general arrangement is found in women's cloths, but the motifs are more naturalistic flowers and plants, animals and birds. The repertoire includes the *tutu* mirror image of a pair of birds with a stylized plant in-between, and the *ledo* snake motif, which is possibly a fertility symbol. The *hebe* and *makuba* floral medallions are thought to have derived from the double-ikat *patola* of India (though there are still many unanswered questions about the to-ing and fro-ing of images between South and South East Asia).

In North and North East Thailand, the *lykhit* (two-colour weave) and *matmee* (ikat) patterns vary from village to village, depending on the cultural origins of the people, and the proximity to the bordering countries, Burma (now called Myanma), Laos and Cambodia (Kampuchea),

OPPOSITE, TOP LEFT: *Binding warp with strips of rubber for ikat, in Koyyalagudem co-operative, South India;* TOP RIGHT: *dyeing the bound warp yarns;* BOTTOM LEFT: *dried yarn after the binder has been removed, revealing the pattern;* BOTTOM RIGHT: *fanning out the warp to separate the threads before tying it through the heddles (the cotton strings which lift the threads).*

RIGHT: *A woman carrying prepared warps home on her back, with ready-tied heddles in her right hand; she can then fix the heddles on her loom at home.*

ABOVE: *Tying in a new warp for the weaver to fix into a loom. Each task in the preparation of the warp prior to weaving involves great skill; it saves much time to divide this work between specialists.*

where similar cloths are produced. What they have in common is that most of the motifs are abstract forms of the local flora and fauna and everyday objects. Every pattern, every technique and every width of cloth has a traditional function, such as the border of a woman's skirt, or a long banner for presentation to the temple on certain festive days of the year.

Nowadays, these traditional elements are increasingly adapted to the requirements of export: more cloth is woven in wider widths, and the patterns which were found in women's breast wrappers, or in men's scarves and sashes, are now

ABOVE: *Brocaded Guatemalan* huipil *(woman's blouse).*

OPPOSITE: *Weaving a narrow belt or ribbon. These strips are woven in the Totonicapan area of Guatemala, to be made into belts in Quetzaltenango. The loom is tensioned by a hip-belt, but the warp threads are threaded through and raised by shafts of a small free-standing loom.*

more flexibly applied and can be used in non-traditional clothing.

Traditional patterns can be a source of local pride and identity, but they cannot always be worn with peace of mind. The weavings of Guatemala have the distinct motifs and colours of each weaver's village, creating spectacular splashes of colour at the local markets. However, for political reasons many of the old village patterns are in danger of being lost as some people dare not be so easily identified. Many old *huipils* (women's blouses) are now being sold to tourists, over-dyed and transformed into patchwork bags.

WEAVING CULTURE

The significance of weaving throughout life is still felt in South East Asia – especially in relation to marriage and other rites of passage. Woven cloth has commonly been presented to important guests, and is still a key element in a young woman's marriage dowry. In many communities, a productive and skilled spinner and weaver may be viewed as an attractive wife, as, in case of necessity, she would be able to contribute to the family's income through her craft.

The people of Sarawak, for instance, still measure their family fortune by the number of textiles and gongs they own. Each longhouse on the island may comprise up to a hundred family areas. These are normally partitioned off with wooden boards; however, whenever there is cause for celebration, the boards are brought forward to the communal space to become the backdrops over which are hung many, many *puas* – blanket-sized ceremonial cloths, more often than not of warp ikat. Yet more *puas* are brought out to cover special possessions, and others are spread over the floor to sit on. Within the patterns of highly stylized plant forms are lizards, birds, fireflies and many other creatures which inhabit the local environment. At one time, these cloths were used for carrying human heads brought home as war trophies; today, however, many are being sold off for cash, in response to the collecting boom in the West, and out of necessity as their traditional livelihoods are becoming harder to maintain.

In the economic and cultural history of North and North East Thailand, weaving has played a vital role. Women weave for around four months

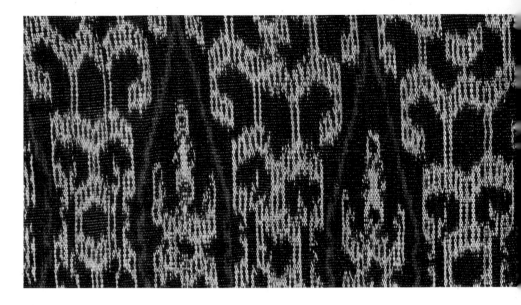

BELOW: Matmee *(weft ikat) from North East Thailand, made with Thai silk in a twill construction, which gives the cloth a marvellous drape and weight.*

of the year, but not in the rainy season (the crucial time for the rice planting), working underneath the living quarters of their raised houses, or in open-sided weaving sheds. Taboos and myths as well as designs have been passed down from mother to daughter through weaving lore. Hand-weaving is strictly women's work; once a man has built the loom, he is not allowed to touch it. Like most producers, the Thais have a rich heritage of weaving and spinning songs, which complement the sounds and rhythms of the craft processes. The lyrics, with suggestive innuendo, play on the opposition of male and female elements built into the cloth. In Thai courtship prose "the finest thread" is a metaphor for a handsome young man, whilst a "twenty-five teeth beater" is the beautiful young weaver of the best silk textile. As well as winning over her beloved, a woman can hope to "make merit" with her weaving. This involves making pillows, sheets and robes for presenting to the monks during Buddhist festivals, an action intended to achieve

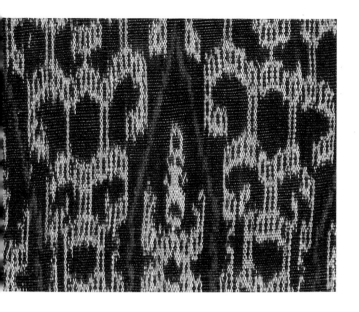

LEFT: *Detail of T'Nalak cloth woven by T'Boli women, who sometimes work images from their dreams into their ikat patterns. These cloths are traditionally used on ceremonial occasions associated with rites of passage (for instance as a blanket for spreading over a woman giving birth to her first child).*

LEFT: *Abaca fibres must be knotted end to end, and stretched out to an even length.*

MIDDLE LEFT: *The warp is bound tightly, using other abaca fibres coated with beeswax (to help resist the colour) for the first stage of dyeing. This is carried out in the kitchen area of the house in two stages: first Kenalum leaves for black, and then Loco roots for red.*

BOTTOM LEFT: *Inserting weft from a long, slim shuttle to make the T'Nalak cloth. To finish, the cloth is beaten with a wooden mallet, then polished with a shell. It takes 3–4 months from start to finish to produce a length of T'Nalak 12 m × 60 cm.*

contentment in this life, and to reach spiritual grace in the next.

The T'Nalak cloth of the T'Boli people in upland Mindanao in the Southern Philippines is highly symbolic and still made using traditional materials, techniques and motifs. Motifs such as snakes and lizards are considered auspicious, especially as symbols of fertility. Like them, T'Nalak cloths were a major part of a woman's dowry and used ceremonially at major points in life; for example, as a blanket to cover the woman when giving birth to her first child.

TAPESTRIES OF LIFE

Weavers in many countries are increasingly focusing their work on wallhangings for the souvenir and export markets, rather than on functional and ceremonial cloths. Today's weavers of Latin America are conscious of their strong tapestry tradition, passed down from ancient prc-Columbian civilizations, when weaving was used for ceremonial and magical garments such as powerful figures of society and shamans would have worn – bearing potent motifs such as the condor, the serpent and abstract figures. The Salasaca Indians, who originate from Bolivia, were already skilled weavers when they settled in Ecuador. Traditionally, their production met their own needs and consisted mostly of striped ponchos and blankets; however, landlessness and deepening poverty mean that today 60% of Salasacas live by commercial craft production – hence the diversification from clothing into bags and wallhangings.

Similarly, in the weaving town of San Pedro de Cajas, 4000 metres up in the Peruvian Andes,

LEFT: *Wool tapestry woven by Salasaca Indians in Ecuador; many colours come from locally available natural dyes, though synthetic dyestuffs are used for blue, green, mauve and orange.*

BELOW: *Peruvian wallhanging; local wool is dyed in the fleece, carded to separate the fibres and arranged into a roll (or rolag). Men do the actual weaving, often with rolags prepared by women. It takes about 2½ days to weave 1 sq.m – much less time than traditional tapestry.*

weaving patterns have changed dramatically. Many weavers continue to produce the traditional *manta* – a striped shawl used by women as baby carriers – but increasingly in cheap factory-spun acrylics, instead of locally available alpaca (some of which now finds its way to the markets of Bolivia). About one-third of the weavers have turned to a new craft, making use of another local raw material – sheep's wool – to weave wallhangings for the tourist and export market.

Weaving activity is at its height after the rainy season, in March and April and then again in June through to November. Every May, the weavers of San Pedro de Cajas set aside their looms to help harvest potatoes, the main crop of the area. However, a large number of weavers have now moved to Lima in search of work, and weave full-time to support their families.

DESIGNS FOR TODAY

Today's designs are as rich and diverse as ever, though some of the traditional motifs have been adapted. Sometimes the colours change to suit Western tastes; some traditional indigo blue and red cloths are now, for instance, being dyed in soft greys and pinks.

Some looms are now being adapted to speed up production. For example, flying shuttles and wider looms have been introduced to weavers in some more commercially minded Thai villages. In Nepal, weavers are also experimenting with wider looms and meterage production, to make the traditional Dhaka cloth into longer more adaptable lengths. Nevertheless making cloth in small lengths is still much more straightforward and familiar to the traditional weaver.

It is important to bear in mind that some things done by hand can never be simulated by machine. Although ikat has been imitated in the West by some extremely sophisticated and expensive warp-printing techniques, the result is but a mere shadow of the real thing. The most complicated computer-based looms cannot reproduce the genuine spontaneity and authentic spirit of cultural tradition taught by example and the result of generations of experience.

RIGHT: *A weaver in Sololà, Guatemala, producing wider cloth than is traditional on a four-shaft treadle loom.*

BELOW LEFT: *The Manipuris of North East India have a tradition of weaving cloth in strong, bright colours with bold stripes.*

BELOW: *Ramchandra Barupal teaching* pattu *weaving to trainees. A* pattu *is a woollen wrap of Rajasthan, India, worn as a shawl or used as a blanket cover during the winter.*

DYEING
AND PRINTING

INDIGO BLUE IS THE UNIVERSAL COLOUR OF WORKWEAR. BRIGHT REDS AND PINKS
ARE SHADES OF YOUTH AND CELEBRATION. THE IMPACT OF COLOUR – THE
MOTIVATION FOR DYEING – HAS DEVELOPED INTO A SYMBOLIC LANGUAGE,
THROUGH WHICH IT IS POSSIBLE TO SIGNIFY AGE, SOCIAL GROUP, AND EVEN
OCCASION. THE PATTERNS WHICH THE DYES BRING TO LIFE MAY BE PRINTED,
PADDED, FOLDED, OR TIED – DEPENDING ON THE TECHNOLOGY AVAILABLE, AND
THE CHEMISTRY OF THE ANIMALS, PLANTS AND MINERALS FROM WHICH THE
COLOURS ARE DERIVED.

ABOVE: *Batik picture on silk, a wallhanging produced at a rehabilitation unit in Mangalore, India.*

OPPOSITE: *A man from Sabu island, Indonesia, wearing batik around his head and a shoulder cloth of cotton ikat dyed with indigo.*

OPPOSITE, BORDER: *Detail of hand-drawn* tulis *batik with shrimp design; Java, Indonesia.*

In these days of mass-manufacture, when the speedy printing of pigment dyes onto cloth needs only a brief, dry heat treatment to fix the colour, it is difficult to appreciate the intricacies of traditional dyeing with extracts of plants, insects, and sea molluscs. In Europe, the medieval layman considered the art of dyeing cloth a magical act – a branch of alchemy. In some traditional societies of the world still, the utmost respect is paid to the indigo dyepot, and an ancient code of cultural taboos is associated with it. Such customs have arisen on opposite sides of the world, apparently independently, yet sharing common characteristics.

READING COLOUR

The significance of colour owes as much to the rarity value, quality and processing of a dyestuff as to the visual impact of its hue. For example, many superstitions are related to indigo, because it is an extremely difficult, unpredictable dye to use. To ensure that the indigo dyepot remains effective and that the colour is evenly distributed, various precautions may be taken during the dyeing process. Both on the Indonesian island of Roti (next to Sumba) and in Yorubaland, Nigeria, a chicken feather is hung over the dyepot to ward off evil spirits. The same idea can be seen on other Indonesian islands, including Sabu; but since the people have become Christianized, in place of the feather a cross is now the protective sign being used.

In many societies, both volatile fashion and long-practised religious customs have responded significantly to the cycle of seasonal change, and of life itself. Bright shades and sombre tones can be expressive of moods considered appropriate to particular occasions and social circumstances. In Rajasthan, during the latter half of the 19th century, the range of tie-dyed patterns on men's turbans was much more varied than today, and the language expressed through them was equally rich. At funeral ceremonies the men wore turbans of subdued mauves and browns with understated tie-dyed spots and checks. While for all occasions widows were required to wear the darker shades of madder red, which is a very fast

dye (referred to as *pakka*, meaning permanent), young people were able to celebrate festivities in bright pinks, hot reds, yellows and lime greens – achieved with synthetic (aniline) dyes imported from Europe. However, these colours were extremely fugitive – in other words, they faded easily in the light and through washing, and were therefore described as *kachcha*. Under the hot sun of the Rajasthani desert they faded within a year, so the clothes had to be re-dyed to look bright and rejuvenated. According to Hindu custom, a new garment should be worn for each religious festival of the calendar, for the sake of ritual purity. Therefore, in recognition of the different characteristics of plant and aniline dyes, the complex rules of observance came to be classified as *pakka* and *kachcha*.

Indigo, the source of blue in true denim, is the most universal of dyes. Its availability and practical advantages (it doubles as an insecticide) are reasons for its common use in work clothing. At the same time, it is a wonderful backcloth for brilliant embroidered colours. In old bedouin dress, as with the embroidered garments of tribal peoples such as the Mien and the Akha, now settled in Northern Thailand, indigo offsets their colourful patterns and coins or other applied metal decoration. Today, however, factory-dyed black cotton, which is perhaps less kind on the eye but more easily obtainable, is often used instead of indigo-dyed cloth.

In Central America, despite the widespread conversion to Catholicism following the Spanish conquest, many beliefs fundamental to the ancient Maya civilization have survived. These include special colour codes, visible in the clothing of the Huichol Indians in Mexico. Blue is the shade of

ABOVE: *A quilt made from cotton waste and tie-dyed cloth; Ahmedabad, India; larger versions of these,* dupattas, *are sold to the local market.*

OPPOSITE: *Blessing the bridegroom – a wedding celebration in Ahmedabad, Gujarat, India, in 1991; she wears a brand-new or newly dyed and printed sari; his turban is made of fine cotton cloth, patterned by folding, rolling and binding the cloth to resist the colour during dyeing – a technique perfected in Rajasthan.*

water; green, the colour of renewal, also refers to the *axis mundi*, the very centre of the Earth. However, the most symbolic colours of all – white, yellow, red and black – correspond to the directions North, South, East, and West, and are also the colours of locally-grown maize. Maize was central to the Mayan – and still today the Huichol – views on life and religion; the maize plant thrives despite areas of poor soil, and, being the staple ingredient in their diet, it is considered the greatest gift the gods ever created.

UNEARTHING EVIDENCE

We cannot determine precisely when dyeing and printing began, though intermittently more archaeological evidence is revealed. Ban Chiang is an ancient funerary site in North East Thailand, where earthenware rollers with impressed patterns have been discovered; these date from about the beginning of the Christian era, and are thought to have been used for decorating cloth. The archaeological evidence of the ancient civilizations of Central and South America reveal splendidly rich patterned fabrics, but nearly all of these were dyed in the yarn before weaving. However, the picture emerging from India is very different, because by 1750 BC at Mohenjo Daro in the Indus Valley the art of making patterns with fast colours on cotton cloth had been developed. India's reputation as a land of master dyers was already well established in the Roman Empire, and by the 5th century AD, Indian cotton cloth was a major international trade commodity, being carried by Arab ships between the Indonesian spice islands, the coasts of Africa, and the Mediterranean.

the Mediterranean and Red Sea ports. Their patterns are mostly in madder red and black on white, occasionally white on indigo blue, and sometimes white on red. What is special about India's early development of dyeing was its achievement in fixing fast, bright colours on cotton – a fibre which is much more difficult to dye than silk or wool.

THE SOURCES OF DYES

Plants and minerals are the most common sources of "natural" dyes, whilst the more prestigious dyes in history come from insects and molluscs. Along the Pacific coast of Mexico lives a species of shellfish called *Purpura patula pansa*. As the name suggests, this is a source of purple. The related Mediterranean species *murex* produced a similar purple, which became a symbol of high rank in imperial Rome. It is very special, maybe because of its intense hue, but particularly because of the limited supplies of the dye and labour-intensive means of extracting it. Occasionally still used by Mexican Indians, the *Purpura patula* is picked off wet rocks at low tide; the dyer squeezes and blows on the mollusc which, in distress, secretes a liquid onto the yarn held against it. Within the next three minutes, the substance turns from transparent to dull yellow, vivid green, and finally purple. The shellfish is then returned to the sea, only to be "milked" again a month later.

Cotton fragments with simple animal, tree of life, and other patterns, believed to originate from the Indian subcontinent, have been found in rubbish tips at Fostat, the medieval city which predates modern Cairo, and in other sites around

ABOVE: *Market scene, San Francisco del Alio, Guatemala; women wear colourful skirts of local ikat cloth.*

The other animal sources are the insect dyes, cochineal and kermes, which are much more widely used than the precious shellfish. The cochineal beetle, or *Coccus cacti*, enjoys the climate of Central and South America where it feeds off

cactus plants belonging to the prickly pear (*Opuntia*) family; the dried bodies of females are used. Related to cochineal, various species of kermes are found in the Mediterranean and Middle East. The colouring matter of both is kermesic acid; but because this is less concentrated in kermes than in cochineal, the latter was imported to Europe in large quantities after Columbus's "discovery" of the New World. All types of this insect can produce a rich range of reds and pinks.

Compared with the insect and shellfish dyes, the sources of vegetable colours are extremely diverse: they include roots, bark, berries, grasses, and leaves, the two most important being madder and indigo. The principal colouring substance in the roots of madder (*Rubia tinctorum*) is alizarin, also present in other plants such as morinda (*Morinda citrifolia*), which has been grown in Indonesia for centuries. Indigotin is the dyestuff extracted from the leaves of indigo-bearing plant species, the main ones being Northern Europe's woad (*Isatis tinctoria*), and various *Indigofera* and *Polygonum* species of much hotter climates.

ABOVE: *Dyes used by the Aabodana women's co-operative group in Sarkhej, Ahmedabad, India: clockwise from top –* bedi *and* himaj *(light yellow), pomegranate (fixer), and* elejerin *(red; a local spelling of alizarin).*

LEFT: *Any old rusty iron goes into the bucket for dyeing.*

RIGHT: *Hajraben rinsing tie-dyed cloth.*

Indigo used to be cultivated and processed on a large commercial scale, and from antiquity until the 19th century, was exported all around the world from producers in the Arab world, Indonesia, India, the West Indies, and Latin America. However, for local craft production, plants indigenous to the region are used and processed on a much smaller scale. For example, the indigo-bearing plants used in North and North East Thailand today are often grown in plots close to the house.

Historically, the most important and widely used mineral has been iron, used both as a dye and as a mordant (a metallic salt in solution which helps to fix a dye such as madder into the fibres). In the past, minerals were dug up from naturally occurring deposits in the soil. In Thailand, for example, yarns used to be immersed in the mud

from buffalo wallows, in order to fix black, blue and some yellow dyes onto cotton. Nowadays, however, anything goes into the bucket, from old bicycle wheels and iron bars to horseshoes, as can be seen in Bagru near Jaipur, and other Indian dyeing centres where some traditional techniques continue, although prepared mordants can easily be bought from the local market.

Initially whatever is to be dyed – fleeces, skeins of yarn, or lengths of cloth – must be washed to remove any resistant lanolin, gum or dirt. For example, cotton fabrics may be scoured in a caustic soda solution, to remove the starch-based size applied to stiffen the threads before weaving. There are many other preparatory processes which help the fibres to take up the colour.

Ingredients used in dyeing include buffalo dung, beeswax, kerosene, mineral salts (most

ABOVE: *Hajraben, Rehana and Zubeda of Aabodana, unfolding a length of tie-dyed cloth to show Uma Swaminathan of the Self-Employed Women's Association (SEWA), working to improve women's income and status, which has played an important role in setting up and supporting the co-operative.*

commonly alum and iron), fruits and molasses, urine, and lyes (strong alkaline solutions) of wood ash – quite apart from the dyestuff. Light, water, and heat are possibly the most vital processing components, and this explains why centres of dyeing developed in hot climates, located close to a flowing river, with space around to lay the cloths out in the sun. Naturally, such conditions mean that production has to cease during the rainy season.

SEEING RED

Madder and cochineal are the great red dyes. To fix the colour into the cloth, not every natural dye requires a mordant – although most do. The most common mordant is iron and alum, although today chromium (highly toxic) is sometimes used

to achieve extra-bright colours. The mordant's function is to encourage the dye to combine with the fibre. The type and strength of mordant used, and even the minerals in the soil where the plant grew, affect the colour and depth of shade. No two fibres will respond in the same way to the same dye recipe, and every dyestuff requires different conditions of temperature, humidity and acidity in order to fix it.

An iron mordant used with madder produces a range of mauves to purple and black; alum, on the other hand, produces soft pinks through to puce and rich reds; a mixture of alum and iron yields shades of brown. Sometimes, depending on fashion and taste, this is intentional, to tone the colours up or down; a highly skilled dyer can intuitively adjust the recipe – just like a good cook. Nevertheless, a "discoloration" occasionally occurs due to the minerals naturally present in the local water supply, which is why the first centres of dyeing were located by rivers with the purest flowing water. These basic principles of adjusting and fixing the colour which apply to madder, are equally applicable to other dyes requiring mordants, including kermes and cochineal, although the resulting colours will be very different.

DYEING THE BLUES

Indigo, on the other hand, needs no mordant for it is a vat dye – and extremely temperamental. Where indigo is prepared for local use, the leaves are picked off the plant and then soaked in a large pot of water, and whisked regularly for some hours, so that oxygen enters the pot and helps the leaves to ferment and decompose. The

ABOVE: *Binding weft threads with strips of plastic before resist-dyeing with indigo to make* matmee *(weft ikat cloth); Sang Sa village, North East Thailand.*

RIGHT: *Anoukien, the quality controller in Sang Sa village, wearing* matmee *and about to dye the tied weft.*

OPPOSITE, TOP LEFT: *Indigo dyeing near Nong Khai, Thailand. To achieve a really deep blue the yarn must be immersed in the dye many times; on contact with the air, the indigo oxidizes into the fibres, turning them from greeny-yellow to blue.*

OPPOSITE, TOP RIGHT: *Hanging skeins of indigo-dyed cotton on a line; the longer the indigo is left, the better it fixes.*

OPPOSITE, BOTTOM: *Untying the resist-binding, revealing the pattern in the natural white.*

weather needs to be hot and humid for this to work. After a few days, once the precipitated indigotin has sunk to the bottom of the pot, dyeing can begin immediately. Alternatively, the water may be drained off, leaving a blue paste which is then kept in a dark, covered pot for future use.

For dyeing, all sorts of ingredients are added to the indigotin to achieve a good degree of alkalinity, and to assist fermentation. The most common are wood-ash lye and lime (for alkalinity), rice wine, urine, dates, or other sweet fruit (for fermentation) – depending on what is available. Each dyer's recipe is a closely guarded secret, and tends to be inherited. Because the fermented indigo in the vat or dyepot is in a reduced state (i.e. without oxygen), cloth must be introduced to it very carefully, letting no air in. When the cloth is drawn out of the pot it looks greenish-yellow; but on contact with oxygen in the air it immediately begins to turn blue – a fascinating process to watch.

To achieve a really deep indigo, verging on black, the cloth may be dipped many times. Therefore in certain cultures of West Africa and the Arab world the darkest cloth and yarn is a status symbol, because it requires much labour and expense. This is also why the deepest blue Persian carpets were the most highly prized.

Indigo dye and resist-dyeing are regular partners in the game of patterning cloth, the reason being that it is extremely difficult to apply indigo directly; if this were done, the dye would oxidize on the brush or other tool somewhere mid-air between the pot and the cloth. It follows that the cloth must be taken to the pot, not vice versa.

RESIST-DYEING

The objective of resist-dyeing is to deny the colour access to certain areas of yarn (in the case of ikat) or woven cloth (in batik, for example). If, for instance, the resist is applied to natural white cotton which is then dyed blue, the pattern will appear in white against a blue background.

There are several ways of achieving this kind of effect. Beeswax is used in Indonesia for batik, and is proving increasingly popular in other countries. Methods of folding, pleating and binding, sometimes combined with dabbing colour directly onto the cloth, are perfected in the turbans of Rajasthan, creating vibrant checks and

TOP: *Detail of a batik sarong with a flower pattern; Sri Lanka.*

ABOVE: *Detail of wax-resist dyed cotton.*

OPPOSITE: *A member of the Sundarban Khadi Village Industrial Society in Calcutta painting wax resist onto cotton.*

zig-zag effects. Blockprinters in Northern India use a clay-based paste resist, whilst the resists of Japan and West Africa are made of rice- and cassava-starch respectively. There is even a method of resisting with stitches, whereby the cloth is either laboriously embroidered (in West Africa, with raffia yarn), or sewn with running stitches and then tightly gathered, only to be unpicked after dyeing. Alternatively, the cloth may be tied around a seed for a spot effect; or groups of threads may be tightly wrapped prior to weaving to create the many variations of warp, weft and double ikat found in Asia and parts of Latin America.

BATIK: DRAWING WITH WAX

Batik is a resist-dyeing process, in which hot wax is applied to cloth (usually fine cotton, but occasionally silk) to stop the colour from penetrating the fibres. The Indonesian island of Java is the home of the most celebrated examples of this craft. Javanese women used to wear *tulis* (hand-drawn) batik for everyday sarongs (wrap-around tubular skirts) but nowadays, although some extremely fine cloths are still being produced, the hand-drawn batik is a luxury reserved for more formal wear with an unstitched skirt wrapper and a short jacket. Men, too, wear it on special occasions; and new *tulis* lengths are purchased especially for events such as circumcision and marriage, when cloth is considered of great significance.

Tulis is the traditional hand-drawn batik made by women in Java using a *canting* – a bamboo pen with a copper spout. The spouts are sometimes multiple, to draw more than one line simultaneously; the gauge of the spout, which varies

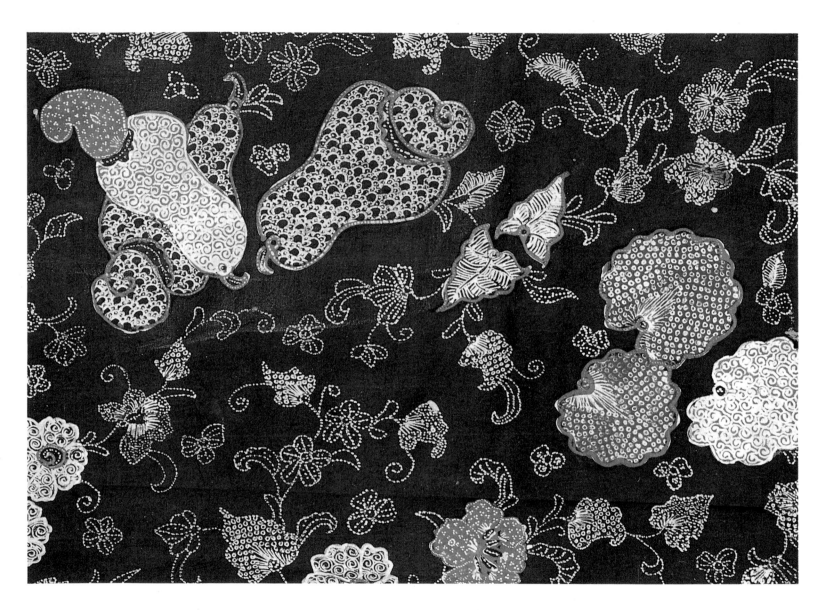

from one *canting* to another, controls the width of the wax line. Machine-printed imitations of *tulis* batik – some of them very convincing – are however now forcing the hand techniques into virtual extinction. Increasingly nowadays more *cap* batik is produced; the wax resist is printed on with a metal stamp (the *cap*). This is mainly men's work, and a much quicker process. (The men

ABOVE: *Detail of hand-drawn batik* (tulis) *sarong from Java.*

tend to produce *cap* batiks in workshops, whereas the women often work in the family compound.) Several stages of waxing are required to produce a cloth with more than one colour; sometimes the final colours are added by brush.

Javanese batik includes a wide range of patterns, including dragons, peonies, the mythical winged Garuda, and the tree of life. Though these

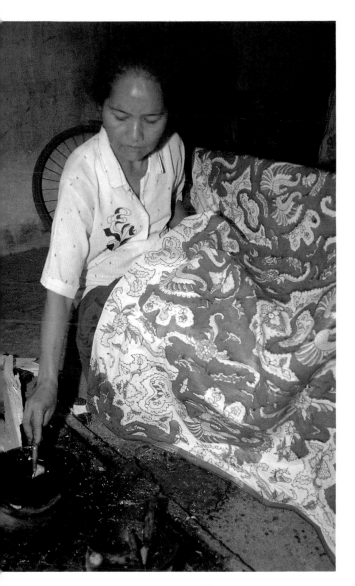

LEFT: *The hand-drawn* tulis *batik of Java is executed by women using a* canting, *a bamboo pen with a copper spout which gradually releases the hot wax. The cloth is draped over a bamboo frame and held at an obtuse angle; in this way, it is much easier to control the flow of wax.*

ABOVE: *Printing batik with a metal stamp or* "cap", *Java, Indonesia; this is always men's work, and is much quicker than painting wax by hand, resulting in a more regular effect.*

ABOVE RIGHT: *Variously patterned* caps *(metal stamps).*

RIGHT: *Dipping the* cap *into the pot of hot wax; kerosene is usually mixed with the wax, the amount used depending on the desired degree of "crackle".*

reflect specific regional styles within Indonesia, many motifs are also derived from Indian, Islamic, European, and Chinese sources, due to the settlement and trading patterns of foreigners over the centuries.

The term *batik* is an Indonesian one, but the wax-resist process is practised extensively in India, in other parts of Asia including Sri Lanka and

Thailand, and in Africa and Latin America. Sales of all crafts are subject to fluctuations brought about by unpredictable changes in local, foreign and tourist markets, and producers of textiles, such as batik, are especially affected by changing taste and fashions in the West. For this reason, the batiks produced by women in Sri Lanka include sarongs for the local market, but also an increasing

number of pictorial wallhangings, which have the advantage of being less susceptible to changes in fashion – a trend which is evident in the work of many producer groups involved in batik.

TIE-AND-DYE

For many people, tie-dyeing conjures up images of hippie T-shirts and the bold scarves of Rajasthan with their primary colours and large spots. But this impression does injustice to the incredibly fine *bandhani* turbans and saris which reflect some of the best Indian craftsmanship. These are usually executed on cotton cloth so fine as to be

ABOVE: *Unravelling the threads from a tie-dyed (bandhani) cloth; made by members of the Social Work and Research Centre. The cloth is dyed and printed in Bagru, near Jaipur, Rajasthan, a town full of blockprinting and dyeing workshops.*

OPPOSITE: *Tree of life batik hanging, drawn with beeswax and dyed with indigo; made by Hmong people, Northern Thailand.*

folded into four layers, which are tied simultaneously to create the most intricate of patterns. There are *bandhani* saris featuring elephants, dancing figures, parrots, and other popular figurative subjects of Hindu tradition. Tiny spots are created by stretching the fabric over a finger-tool resembling a pointed thimble, and binding the tip with thread before resist-dyeing; sometimes boards, with nails hammered into patterns, are used instead.

Today, a number of tie-dyed cottons for clothing and household use are produced in East Africa. The craft is recent, introduced from the Indian sub-continent or from Indonesia as a

result of trade, and particularly since the settlement of Asians in East Africa. (There is a longer tradition of resist-dyed cloths in West Africa.) Many workshops were set up in the 1960s and 1970s in response to fashion trends. Because tie-dyeing in its basic form can be one of the simplest textile techniques, needing very little equipment and not requiring a very long period of training, it has been seen as an appropriate craft to introduce to income-generating projects.

BLOCKPRINTING

Printing is a form of localized dyeing – and since India mastered the application of mordants on selected areas of cloth, it is also the home of master blockprinters. The appearance of the finished cloth depends on many factors, including the condition of the woodblock and quality of its carving; how evenly the cloth is laid on the print table; and the degree of accuracy with which the block is registered (matched to the neighbouring unit of repeat in the pattern).

The "mordant style" of printing, which entails printing the pattern in a paste containing mineral salts and then immersing the whole cloth in dye, creates typical Indian patterns dominated by madder red and black. To achieve black and red patterns on a white background, the outline block is usually used first, to apply the iron mordant. This immediately reacts with an ingredient introduced to the cloth at a preparatory stage (usually tannic acid from the myrabolan fruit, a kind of cherry). Then the alum mordant (for red details) is printed with a second block. The whole cloth is then immersed in a madder dyebath. Where there is alum, a deep, fast red will be fixed into

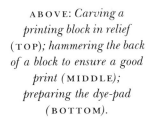

ABOVE: *Carving a printing block in relief* (TOP)*; hammering the back of a block to ensure a good print* (MIDDLE)*; preparing the dye-pad* (BOTTOM)*.*

ABOVE RIGHT: *Rehana blockprinting; though women work with smaller blocks, they may suffer from painful wrists because of the impact of hitting the back of the block so hard; Ahmedabad, India.*

the cloth, and where iron mordant has been printed it will create a strong black. The whole black and red cloth must then be rinsed, and rinsed again in a bath of dung in water to remove any colour residue and clear the unmordanted areas to reveal the natural white of the cloth.

Printing in the mordant style is often combined with resist-dyeing. Iron mordant is printed with the first block, and a wax resist is applied second, before the whole cloth is dyed in madder to create a pattern in white with a black outline on a red background. Only one application of dye is thus needed.

If the design features small details in blue, traditionally the entire cloth, except for those details, is painted with beeswax and then immersed in the indigo vat, followed by lengthy and sometimes repeated dipping, hanging, rinsing and drying. However, some cloths are now painted or printed directly with blue instead. For green, the process of printing or painting with alum begins all over again, on top of a mid-blue colour, and the cloth is sent to a yellow dyebath. These procedures were followed to produce the finely painted, multi-coloured chintzes which were exported to the West in the 17th and 18th centuries.

Traditionally, blockprinting is men's work, but now more women are practising the craft. One example of this is in Bangladesh, which has not previously had any blockprinting tradition. Though tie-dyeing and printing are normally distinct professions, more recently – to minimize the enormous drop in earnings during the monsoon season – some women in India have diversified, in order to work throughout the year. Thus they tie cloth for *bandhani* during the monsoon, and print and dye when the weather is dry.

NATURAL VERSUS SYNTHETIC

Ironically perhaps, most "natural" dyeing today involves the products of the European chemical industry – namely, alizarin, which was synthesized in 1868, and synthetic indigo, developed in 1880. At the time when the British scientist William Perkin discovered aniline mauve in 1856, around 300 brands of Bengal indigo were on the market. We can calculate that, if indigo had not been synthesized, in order to satisfy world

ABOVE: *Swatches of blockprinted cotton to be made into clothing; Kathmandu, Nepal.*

ABOVE RIGHT: *Placing a piece of paper at a 45-degree angle; this will partially mask the block to achieve a mitred border at the corner; Nepal.*

demand, by the end of the 19th century half of India's soil would have been dedicated to its production! If one also contemplates the labour involved in indigo cultivation (which was once the work of slaves), it is not surprising that ready-made packets of dye in powder form are locally favoured, and that in place of real madder and indigo the synthesized versions of these are used.

Nonetheless, though convenient, synthetic dyes can be difficult and costly to obtain. For instance, in Malawi during 1988 the cost of dyes doubled, and synthetic black was unobtainable. To improve the colour-fastness, one tie-and-dye workshop

consumerism, in fact *all* plant and protein dyes require a finely tuned understanding of chemical change. Plant dyes can sometimes be used unwisely – for example, used in combination with a chrome mordant, they are extremely hazardous. Also, all dyes are responsive to changes of atmosphere, not just the extremes of blistering dry heat and torrential rain, but also more subtle changes of weather from one hour to the next. Using chemical dyes does not in fact compensate for these weather conditions. In some respects, they are even more temperamental than plant dyes, because they have been developed for use with uniform qualities of cloth in controlled factory conditions; the majority of dyeing and printing in the developing world takes place outdoors, or in open-sided workshops, and so commercial dyes are often less appropriate than the local plant ones they have replaced. Another problem is that dyers may be unable to read the manufacturer's instructions, which can lead to dangerous mis-use and poor fastness unless the dyers receive specific training in the use of the dye products.

would have liked to use more hot dyes than cold. This was a problem, for many hot dyes need to be fixed with caustic soda, of which there was also a shortage. For these reasons, the producers investigated natural dyeing.

The healing properties of certain natural dyes offer many advantages. For example, turmeric, with which a range of yellows can be dyed, is commonly used in India as an antiseptic, just as indigo and woad have been all over the world. The creamy background colour in some block-printed cottons is achieved with *harar*, a herb also used as a laxative. And, on an environmental note, waste from natural dyeplants can be used as organic fertilizers.

Though commercially manufactured dyes tend to be singled out as *chemical*, and are perceived therefore as noxious synthetics which harm our environment, and the *natural* dyestuffs have taken on a new significance in the age of green

ABOVE: *Chemically dyed alpaca yarns drying in Bolivia; the subdued shades imitate natural dyes.*

OPPOSITE: *Blockprinted cottons spread out in the sun to help fix the colours; produced by the Women's Skill Development project in Kathmandu, Nepal.*

RECENT TRENDS

Technology is getting more sophisticated and easier to master. Pigments are about the simplest colourants to use today, and require none of the to-ing and fro-ing between the dyebath, river or tank for washing and rinsing, or sun-drenched ground for fixing and drying. A pigment is a colour in powder form, which is mixed with a thickening emulsion and binder into the correct consistency for printing. It is applied directly to dry cloth, and can then be fixed by heat.

At a women's income-generating project in Manikganj, Bangladesh, some printing is being done with pigments and blocks. The cloths were once spread out on the roof of the building in the sun for five or six days; but now they are much more efficiently and reliably fixed in a gas-fired baker (a hot cupboard) into which the cloth is fed over and under a series of rollers. This can be used irrespective of the weather, creating the potential for year-round income.

An increasing number of textile workshops, some old, many new, are printing with screens. Screen-printing with pigments generally requires less skill and time than the older methods do. Being a relatively new technology, it is usually men who are committed to using this technique. Understandably, it is tempting to switch to such a "direct style" of printing, in order to make a decent living from printing cloth. Besides, if the average Western consumer does not really appreciate the lengthy procedures involved in the best blockprinting and natural dyeing, there is little professional incentive for the blockmaker and -printer to continue their craft.

So, on the one hand there are plans to create employment for more people through the re-vived cultivation of indigenous dyeplants, the secrets of which are kept in the memories and fingers of a very few older men and women, whose knowledge is highly valued. On the other hand, more modern (though still intermediate) technologies and materials are being introduced, to generate income all year round. It would seem that, in India at least, the ancient crafts of block-printing and natural dyeing, traditionally prac-tised by men, are now being seriously challenged by pigments, synthetics, screens, and women.

EMBROIDERY
AND APPLIQUE

WITHIN THE WORLD OF EMBROIDERY AND APPLIQUE EXIST SOME OF THE MOST
DRAMATIC AND PERSONAL FORMS OF DECORATION AND CELEBRATION. FROM
PATTERNS INTRICATELY BUILT OUT OF TINY STITCHES TO MUCH BOLDER ONES
CREATED FROM SCRAPS OF CLOTH, THE RESULTS OFTEN ZING WITH COLOUR. THE
MOST PROLIFIC MOTIFS ARE FLOWERS – BURSTING SPRIGS, TRAILING VINES, AND
SCATTERED PETALS OF DIFFERENT COLOURS. WHETHER IN A BARREN DESERT
LANDSCAPE OR IN HARSH MOUNTAIN REGIONS, THEY ARE OFTEN REMINDERS –
VISUALLY AND SYMBOLICALLY – OF FRESHNESS AND ABUNDANCE.

ABOVE: *Detail of a* mola
*reverse appliqué panel,
made by Cuna Indians.*

OPPOSITE: *A Mien child
in an embroidered carrying
sling, Nam Ki village,
Northern Thailand; the hat
is decorated to make it look
like a flower. Children are
thought to be flower spirits.*

OPPOSITE, BORDER: *A
Hmong appliqué collar.*

Many stitching techniques probably first began as methods of sewing and mending, before developing into their own rich, decorative vocabulary. Quilting started as a means of joining layers of cloth together for warmth and protection, and whilst much of the Bangladeshi women's *kantha* work still fulfils these functions, with its layering of old pieces of cloth, the strongest impression is of its superb decorative qualities, and of its varied pictorial composition and range of stitches.

A seam can also be turned into a colourful detail of clothing; some of the indigo blue skirts worn by Guatemalan women are constructed from just two pieces, joined horizontally across the middle by closely worked binding stitches in a rainbow of colours, resembling a rich braid. The skirts of the Rabari women in Gujarat, Western India, on the other hand, often feature motifs in an interlaced stitch which is rather like darning in mid-air, while in Northern Thailand the various subgroups of the Lahu people can be distinguished by the colour and arrangement of cloth strips applied to their jackets on the sleeves. These act as a striking code of identification, as well as being decorative, though the patches of printed cloth which embellish the sides of the garment have an additional function – to reinforce the openings at the hips.

THE FUNCTION
OF EMBROIDERY

Embroidery is fundamental to many cultures. In many languages of the world even the words for "flowers", "rivers" and "streams" also mean "embroidery". However, there are also some cultures which have no embroidery tradition – possibly for practical reasons. Embroidery stitches and layers of appliqué add one, if not two (front and back) layers to the cloth; this increased weight would be physically stifling to wear in the tropical climates of Africa and Asia, and so embroidered clothing is less prevalent in such regions. Nevertheless, even if embroidery is not part of common dress, cloths for special occasions may be decorated – as a mark of honour and for dramatic visual effect. In India, items such as

bridal canopies and tent-covers for buffalo-carts decorated with appliqué shield whomever sits beneath them from the burning rays of the sun and make a bold impact in procession. And amongst the peoples of Nigeria, appliqué in the broadest sense (of cloth, beads, amulets and other magical attachments) indicates a person of particular importance, and pictorial appliqué has been used in Annang shrine cloths to honour the dead.

Where embroidery does not appear to complement the climate, or where it supersedes weaving, it may well have been introduced from another culture. It was the Spanish who introduced satin-stitch embroidery to Central America; in some cases, this has superseded the intricate woven decoration of women's *huipils* (blouses), and distinctions of pattern between one village and the next may not be so clear as in the past, because of this cultural "interference".

ABOVE LEFT: *Man embroidering* aari *in Kaurala village; an* ari *(tambour hook) is lying by his right hand. There are about 80–90* aari *producers in the village.*

ABOVE: *A bride's sari embroidered with* zari *work, worn at her wedding by a woman from Ahmedabad, Gujarat, India.*

RIGHT: *A troupe of entertainers, just outside New Delhi: applied metal discs and* zari *embroidery decorate the men's jackets. A number of projects have number of projects have been set up to support such magicians, dancers and acrobats.*

TOP: *Lahu women in Northern Thailand; one weaves cloth on a body-tensioned loom.*

ABOVE: *Detail of banded decoration on the sleeve of a Lahu Sheh Leh jacket, and showing appliqué work of printed cloth reinforcing the side seam. There are a number of sub-groups of the Lahu people in Thailand; the clothes of each are identifiable.*

In the hills of Northern Thailand, needlework still plays a role in the lives of tribal peoples. Here, colours, stitches and patterns are as much a part of language as the words of a sentence. There may even be inflections of meaning or indications of temperament in the tension of the stitches, or in the focus on detail. For this reason, the inspection of a young Mien woman's embroidery skills by her prospective family-in-law will affect the bridal price, and will even influence their judgement of her reliability as future wife and mother. Differences of age and marital status can also be read from the proportions of colour and decorative details. The batik skirts of Hmong women and girls are finely pleated and decorated around the hem with a combination of cross-stitch and appliqué – the younger the wearer, the deeper and more brightly coloured the border. This distinction falls into a pattern common to many folk dress traditions

were destroyed by war, continue to practise their counted-thread embroidery there. Two of the main types are *graphdozi* (a cross-stitch) and *tar-shumar* (literally meaning "counting thread"), a closely worked short stitch creating a brick effect. The producers say that *graphdozi* is easier to learn, but more time-consuming to execute. In Akora Khattak refugee camp, several different tribal groups are represented. Many of these refugees have come from tribes that were originally located in the area of the great silk route, which connected the great trading nations of the West and the Middle East on the one hand, and India and China on the other. Both the patterns and the materials of their cloths reflect this long history of cultural contact through the exchange of goods and migration.

These various cultural histories are reflected in the different patterns and techniques of their stitches. Simple intersected diamond patterns of alternating colours are made by women of Pashtun and Tadjik origin from Kandahar Province,

around the world, including some rural communities of Eastern Europe – that is, bright reds and pinks are associated with youth; but later in life a greater proportion of dark colours is worn.

COUNTING THREADS

Cross- and darning-stitches involve counting a certain number of threads in the cloth between each stitch, so that the needle is inserted at very regular intervals. Both of these techniques offer a variety of geometrical effects, resulting in designs which often relate to the weaving and carpet knotting of the same region or culture. The work is not over-figurative: occasionally birds and beasts are identified simply by a camel's hump or a peacock's tail, but mostly the motifs are stylizations whose origins are only revealed by the name of the stitch.

Afghan refugees, who fled to the North West Frontier Province of Pakistan after their villages

ABOVE LEFT: *An Akha girl's hat, Northern Thailand: the stages of development from adolescence to womanhood are marked by the ceremonial adding of Job's tears (seeds from a local, annual tropical grass), red and white beads, and silver coins to various items of clothing.*

ABOVE: *Detail of a Karen waistcoat front, with Job's tears embroidery; in tribal villages of Northern Thailand, such decorations are offset by the red and deep indigo of blouses, hats and belts. Shells from the coast are considered particularly propitious, but if a girl cannot afford cowries, Job's tears are used instead.*

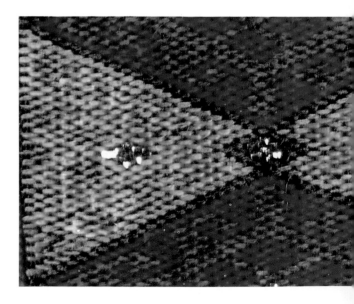

whereas the Hazara people within the camp derive their designs from a Turkoman tribe in the Ghazni area with whom they once had contact.

These kinds of silk embroidery from Central Asia were once used to embellish exquisite coats, and colourful silk tufts would trim the edges of purses. Today, cotton cloth from Lahore, dyed black, and silk and gold thread produced by mills in other parts of Pakistan, are brought into the camps for embroidery use. This enables the refugee women to maintain some of their cultural identity and creative expression, whilst producing items for which there is a steady market.

MAD ABOUT NEEDLEWORK

Some of the most exquisite cross-stitch embroidery identifies and decorates the dress of the Mien and the Hmong tribal people in Northern Thailand. Though the overall effect of each group's patterns is distinctive, they share similar motifs. This indicates the close historical relationship

ABOVE: *An Afghan graphdozi (cross-stitch) hat worn by Afghan boys, made from factory-spun and -dyed cotton yarns bought in from the textile mills of Pakistan.*

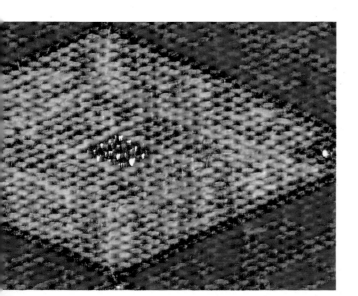

LEFT: Tarshumar *(darning) stitch in silk and gold thread on black cotton, made in an Afghan refugee camp in North West Pakistan. A Danish agency for refugees provides employment for women in the camps, where embroidery reflecting the people's tribal identity and history boosts their morale, as well as generating income.*

between the two groups, whose ancestry lies in Southern China but who have migrated to Thailand during this century.

However, although they use the same stitch, their methods of working are different. The Hmong work with the upper face of the cloth toward them, whereas the Mien embroider from the reverse, which helps to keep the stitches clean. The work is additionally protected by a cloth bag, roughly stitched over the dark areas that are not being worked, so Mien women are able to go about their business, continually stitching, either sitting or standing – often with a baby on the back in an embroidered carrier. They have an expression "*Mauq Zovj*", meaning that they "are crazy about embroidery" – and one pair of trousers after another is produced (though each one may take six months to complete), as their creative work is slotted in between various daily tasks. Other items of embroidered clothing are turbans, waist sashes, and children's hats.

A look at the Mien's attitude towards their craft and the patterns worked in it offers a delightful insight into embroidery's role in folklore. The Mien worship their ancestral spirits and also practise a form of Taoism. Since embroidery is a key aspect of their cultural identity and belief system, it is used as a metaphor in their creation myths. One explains the formation of the Thai hillsides they now inhabit: a sister, Faam Tah, and her brother, Faam Kah, made the earth, the sky, and the Mien people. Faam Tah created an expansive land; but her brother, being rather lazy, did not make the sky big enough. So Faam Tah took out her needle and pulled at her thread, piecing and stitching the land into ruffles and pleats of hills and mountains.

The first steps of embroidery are just five motifs, placed around the bottom of the trouser legs, which Mien girls are taught at a young age. As they become more proficient, so they learn more stitches. One, *The Umbrella of Faam Ts'ing*, recalls the flood story in which the Mien were protected from the rain by the umbrella of Faam Ts'ing ("The Three Pure Ones"). The *Python Skin* design resembles a rainbow: this may allude to the legend of Jung Hung, the dragon-king and gatekeeper of heaven, who had forecast that there would be no rain; when he was proved wrong, and the torrents turned to flood, Jung Hung was exiled to earth. The rainbow signifies the dragon's struggle to return to heaven.

The *Tiger Claw* design is frequently found on the Mien children's pompom hats – it is also secretly called *Lovers' Embrace*. This is the stitch referred to in a song about a young girl who daydreams over her stitches as childhood fades away and womanhood approaches:

"I've embroidered
The Lovers' Embrace design.
The *lien peing* flowers
Have already lost their fragrance.
I still wonder to myself
Whose embrace are they . . ."

Traditionally, a boy gives a girl enough cloth to make wedding clothes for them both. On an auspicious day she will begin embroidering them; she may be engaged for months finishing the trousers for herself and possibly for her future mother-in-law, as well as an embroidered sash for her fiancé, and embroidered scarves for the two of them.

ABOVE: *Koi Hient Saeturn wearing embroidered trousers in Nam Ki village, Northern Thailand. Her headdress is embroidered with cross-stitch. Though motifs change very gradually, colours go in fashions – lime green has been popular recently.*

RIGHT: *A Mien woman embroidering, with a baby on her back. Nam Ki village was established in 1950 as a base for some Mien people who had previously been shifting cultivators.*

PAINTING WITH THE NEEDLE

In cross- and darning stitches, the gauge of the needlework is influenced by the fineness and balance of the woven cloth. Embroidery can, on the other hand, work as freely as a brushstroke.

Sometimes the outline is drawn with a chain of stitches, to map out the main shapes. This is more or less how the embroidered *chicnaya* pictures of Peru are made, by both men and women. Using undyed cream-coloured woollen cloth as the background, various natural shades of alpaca yarn are worked in chain stitch. These *chicnayas* feature scenes of everyday Peruvian life, and images such as alpaca which foreign buyers immediately associate with Andean culture.

Compared with the tonal effect of the Peruvian work, with its subtle shades of alpaca, the bright colours of the embroidered panels of Ethiopia are especially striking, with outline stitches and infill of contrasting colours. Their figurative subjects are icon-like, though sometimes they use symmetrical patterns such as the Ethiopian cross and other designs which resemble the facial tattoos of tribes living in the region.

The outline of a design can be filled in with a variety of stitches, both long and short. Unimpeded by line, but guided by a roughly drawn or traced pattern on the cloth beneath, bold executions of satin stitch create an unrestricted splash of colour; by embroidering a hatched effect with two colours a third may be optically mixed, giving a lively three-dimensional illusion. Today's Guatemalan embroidery owes its technique to the Spanish, but the motifs are derived from different phases of their cultural history. Images such as the peacock date from after the Conquest, and enjoy lively interplay with other images that have their origins in the old Mayan civilization, such as the condor (sometimes interpreted as the Imperial double-headed eagle). There is no limit to the vivid colours chosen by the embroiderers, and the possibilities are endless.

TOP: Chicnaya *cushion cover, embroidered in chain-stitch, using a variety of natural alpaca colours; made by a member of the Asociacion Tipu Amaru in Peru.*

ABOVE: *A King David picture, from Ethiopia, made by women in Adi Haki village. The subject matter reflects the strong Christian heritage of the country.*

ABOVE RIGHT: *Length of Guatemalan cloth, embroidered by groups of widows and displaced people.*

KANTHAS OF BENGAL

A lively sense of movement darts around the *kantha* work of Bengali women in Bangladesh. Their running and filling stitches now tend to be sewn through a double layer of cotton, mainly

because of the Western market they are destined for, which demands cushion covers and wall-hangings. However, the art originated as a means of quilting soft, worn-out layers and patches of saris, the stitching being worked in threads unravelled from their coloured woven borders.

The *kantha* is said to represent a wholeness and sense of unity, because it is constructed harmoniously from different parts, rather like the pieced robes of Buddhist monks. The Lord Buddha – and following his path towards enlightenment, many Buddhist priests – wears robes made of rags, as do some ascetics amongst the Buddhist and Muslim communities of Bangladesh. There is a small pantheon of gods and Muslim saints (called *pirs*) who are identified by their rags; one of these is Chindia Dev (meaning Rag God), who is allied to the rag-picking caste.

During this century, factory-spun mercerized

ABOVE LEFT: *Tracing out a cushion cover design for a* kantha, *in Pathalia village, Bangladesh.*

ABOVE: *Working collectively on one* kantha *quilt. Pathalia village has three* jubika (*meaning "life") sub-centres organized by Bangladesh Rural Advancement Committee (BRAC). The women are all landless, and the objective is to give each of them at least enough work for 90 days per year.*

OPPOSITE: *Embroidering a* kantha – *elephants are always popular with the overseas market.*

cotton yarns have been used instead of the threads pulled out of the old sari borders, and the women work on new whole pieces of cloth; the art has lost its old make-do-and-mend quality. Nevertheless, the best *kantha* pieces are still highly creative, especially when a skilled embroiderer is granted freedom to express whatever she observes. However, more often than not, the desperate need to generate income means adhering to the standard traced designs which Western customers find appealing, such as elephants, and figures smoking hukkas. At the same time more buyers are showing interest in the truly original *kanthas*. A positive outcome of all this is that many old designs, once lost through lack of continuity from maker to maker, are being re-introduced. To this end, museum visits are being organized for the producers to study examples of their rich heritage.

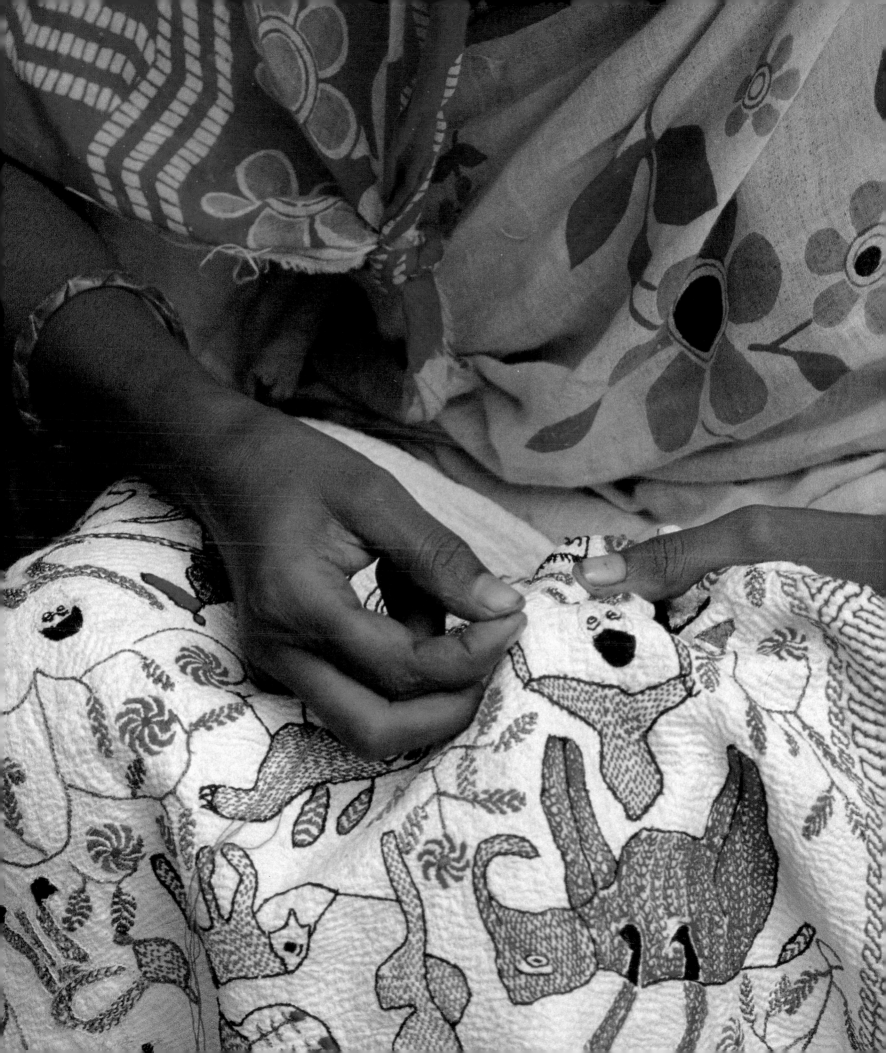

LEFT: Kantha *panel: this is worked with a double thickness of cloth for use as a picture or cushion cover for the Western market. Originally running stitches held together several layers of used cloth to make a* kantha *quilt.*

"The scene on the boat is one of confident and relaxed luxury. It is of course a fantasy, for such wealth and opportunity are impossible for the village craftswoman who envisioned it. Yet it does not stop her from providing all the elements of romance and adventure. After all, a fantasy does not simply relieve you from the humdrum of everyday life, but also sings a requiem for something which can never be." (Joya Pati, of Kumudini Welfare Trust, Bangladesh.)

There is a general acceptance that *kanthas* should not be used by the maker, but be given away. Indeed, they were originally made as a gift, for special occasions such as marriage. Many of the motifs are considered especially appropriate and auspicious for particular occasions: on a wedding quilt, for example, the centre frequently features a mandala (lotus with a thousand petals) shape, which represents the universe. The lotus flower, which opens with the sun, signifies the dawn of the universe. A wheel, a fish, a winnowing fan, and the typical heart-shaped leaves, are all symbols of plenty. A tree of life marks each corner, representing the directions of the wind, or the four phases of life – childhood, adolescence, youth and old age. Exactly how these are interpreted and arranged, and the density and choice of colours, will vary according to region and religion.

Some of the older *kanthas* include images of village folk enjoying a wedding celebration, built into the cloth which itself becomes a focal point of the bridal procession. The *palki*, a canopy cloth, is now sold as a figurative wallhanging, but was once used to cover the palanquin carrying the bride to the groom's house. Other uses of *kanthas* include small envelope shapes to enclose money, prayer mats, covers for plates and dishes, and pillowslips.

Women work together in groups and, depending on the size of the piece, several may share the image-making on a quilt. They tend to work outdoors, their backs supported by the doorpost or wall of a house, in a squatting position which enables them to drape the work over their knees – a natural, human embroidery frame. This art is still a village-based, domestic activity, even though it has now become more commercialized.

Kantha-making on a local commercial level does have historical roots, for village people used to make bed quilts for the landowners of Bengal. The war with Pakistan and subsequent independence changed all that, however, as many women found themselves widowed and separated from their families. A solution was found in the early 1970s with the formation of the first co-operatives of *kantha* makers, and since then, hundreds if not thousands of women have worked collectively in several rural areas of the country. Although the women's designs are now mostly conditioned by the client's orders, and their expression is limited to standardized themes and forms, there is new-found confidence in the independence which generated income can bring; this in turn may lead to greater freedom and creativity.

Although *kantha* work has become internationally associated with Bangladesh (especially since the country's independence in 1971), it

is in fact practised to a greater or lesser extent wherever Bengali women live and continue to express their own culture. This includes West Bengal and Bihar in India, and there is also now a conscious revival of *kantha* work in Bengali communities outside the Indian subcontinent – in some cities in Britain, for instance.

GOLD AND BEADS

Embroidery can affect the shape of a garment and the way it hangs – especially when it employs metal threads or beads. The *zari* (gold thread) work of India is used on areas such as sari borders and the front panels and hems of waistcoats and jackets. Clothes richly decorated with gold thread belong to a long tradition; they are mentioned in classical Sanskrit plays. Much of today's *zari* embroidery is produced by Muslim family groups, within which men are the principal producers, doing the creative and skilled work.

LEFT: Zari *and beadwork being produced by a member of Pushpanjali co-operative, Agra, Northern India. Beads are applied in the space between lines of gold thread embroidery.*

BELOW: *Father and son doing* zari *embroidery. The main centres for the manufacture of* zari *thread are Varanasi and Surat; once it was made of pure silver and gold, now copper electroplated with silver is the standard "imitation". It has escalated in price in recent years, which is partly why the second-hand* zari *trade is thriving; in the city of Ahmedabad there is one particular street where old* zari *saris are bought for unravelling and re-use.*

The women's role on the other hand tends to be restricted to the attachment of handles and straps of bags and purses, with little input in design and marketing.

Zari is the general term for gold thread. However, the threads have many different thicknesses, degrees of brightness, and textures – each of which has a specific name and application. The wider ones tend to be used around the edges of a piece of work, whereas thinner ones are used for finer details such as tassels, or for weaving into the borders of saris and turbans. *Zardozi* is the name given to heavier, more elaborate work applied to cushions, coats, canopies, shoes and animal trappings. *Kamdani* is much lighter in weight, and is appropriate for veils, scarves and caps. Originally a very important industry, *zari* production is still practised in many Indian cities, such as Agra, some with a particular specialism – for example, the neat, glittering bags called

broidered items for their dowries, took up the beadwork in its place. Used in folk embroidery, the beads (nowadays plastic, rather than glass) are often in bright, primary colours with a white background. However, in the *zari* workshops' beadwork and sequinned fabrics, the emphasis is more on differences of lustre and the reflection of light rather than dramatic contrasts of colour.

MIRRORWORK

batwas of Bhopal in Madhya Pradesh. But little real gold and silver is used now; electroplated synthetics have taken over.

Beadwork is closely related to *zari* and glittering versions of it are often produced in the same workshops. The history of the craft is relatively short, however. During the 19th century, Indian traders based in Zanzibar were involved with trade in East Africa. They began to ship back to their native Kutch and Saurashtra opaque and translucent Venetian glass beads, which had been trade goods in Africa for a long while, and where they were applied to crowns, aprons, flywhisks and other regalia of chiefs and kings.

In India, there are two distinctive types of beadwork. On the one hand, there is the sparkling *zari* work produced professionally by men, and on the other, the folk tradition of primary reds and yellows on white, now practised by women for their own use. In Western India, it was initially the craftsmen of the Mochi (cobbler) caste who applied the beads, but before long these professionals began to embroider for the women of the Kathiawar peninsula, who, as they gradually ceased producing all their own em-

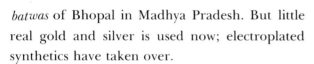

ABOVE LEFT: *Lakshmi Ben cutting up mirrors for* abhala *work. She works in-between household jobs, cutting through about 1 kilo of mirror per day; her daughter works at this as well, and the younger children help out after school to contribute to the family's income.*

ABOVE: *Sampler showing progressive stages of buttonhole stitch used to secure the mirror discs in place; from St Mary's, Ahmedabad, India. Mirrors are used to emphasize features such as animals' eyes and the centres of flowers. Mirrorwork often incorporates stitches developed by distinct tribal groups, such as the Rabari's interlacing-stitch, though most women working for St Mary's are from low-caste Bankar and Chamar families from drought-ridden Saurashtra.*

Mirrorwork, known in India as *abhala*, is a sparkling combination of small round mirrors, framed and held in place by buttonhole stitches, and a rich variety of embroidery techniques worked in bright silk threads. Once, the desert of Western India was the natural source of reflective mica, from which the mirrors were made; then glass was used, but the modern equivalent is a laminate which can be scissored into shape.

Abhala reflects any light in dark interiors, and shimmers like a mirage in the blazing sun. Some very fine examples of this technique are the wedding shawls of the Rabari shepherd caste in Sind and Gujarat with their deep red cloth backgrounds. *Abhala* also features in many aspects of decoration in Gujarati houses. The first colourful item to greet the visitor is a *toran*, a panel which hangs over the doorway as a good omen. Other items of mirrorwork are large rectangular wallhangings called *chandrawas*, and smaller square pieces (*chaklas*) used to cover pieces of furniture. The panels of some chests and cupboards also glisten with the same mirror theme. The overall effect is to lighten up an otherwise dark interior, for the windows are few and small.

LEFT: *Detail of a* chakla, *an embroidered panel used to wrap round a bride's dowry articles and later hung in the home.*

RIGHT: *Traditional embroidery of Banaskantha district in the north of Gujarat.*

BELOW: *Detail of a* toran *(door frieze) from Gujarat.*

APPLIQUE

Though the basic idea of appliqué is to apply a patch onto a larger piece of cloth, there are many variations on the theme. Virtually anything can, and has been applied to cloth, from the shocking pink feathers on a teenage Akha girl's hat to heavy metal discs and coins, pompoms and shells – even discarded metal zips on an Indian boy's cap. In Nepal, thick threads may be simultaneously twisted and applied to blockprinted fabrics. On the appliqué jacket backs of Akha women, threads are couched around the raw edges of applied cloth triangles no more than 2 cm high, emphasizing their shape while also offering resistance to fraying.

Appliqué can be found in many regions of India, especially in dramatic and bold items for household use, such as bedspreads, and also in canopies and tents for great ceremonies and festivals. In embroidery-rich Gujarat, the term *katab* is used, possibly deriving from the English "cut up"; in fact, the British presence in India might well have either initiated or reintroduced an old art of applying cloth. Sometimes this is restricted to the border of a Rabari woman's skirt and combined with embroidery stitches; at other times it is used for enormous canopies, bullock cart covers, and panels in processions and places where the throngs of thousands of devout, festive Indians would not see intricacies of more detailed embroidery. The boldness of scale is dramatically emphasized by strong contrasts of colour: for example, in Gujarat, brilliant shades of primary red, blue, and yellow against white. This effect is sometimes achieved with a combination of direct and reverse appliqué, creating an ingenious sense

The mirrorwork now being made in and around Ahmedabad is based on the work of pastoral communities of Gujarat, Rajasthan, and Sind (now in Pakistan), both content and style depending on which part of West or North West India the embroiderer comes from. Popular images include cows, flowers, parrots, and other exuberant or geometric motifs, but probably the best-loved Hindu folk image of all is Ganesh, the benevolent elephant-headed god who is usually accompanied by his consort, a little rat.

ABOVE: *Aphiku Shermur, wife of the headman, in Saen Charoen village, Northern Thailand, wearing traditional Akha dress of indigo-dyed cloth, with embroidered shoulder bag, appliqué leggings and a hat covered with red wool tassels and metal coins; her jacket back is richly decorated with appliqué. Most of a person's wealth is worn, especially on the headdress: the better-off members of the community wear larger coins of real silver, such as Indian rupees and Chinese dollars.*

ABOVE LEFT: *Detail of appliquéd Akha jacket back.*

of counter-change: positive red on white, and white revealing red beneath.

Reverse appliqué is also used to striking effect in the *mola* (meaning "cloth") work of the Cuna Indians in Panama and Colombia. This involves applying layers of cloth onto a backing, then cutting away shapes to reveal the contrasting colours beneath. Beginning with the bottom layer of fabric, cut-out shapes in different colours are applied and tacked down, layer on layer, and finally the top surface is laid in yet another colour;

ABOVE: *Elephants and castle appliqué hanging, made by women in Barmer district, India, close to the border with Pakistan. Cloth and embroidery thread are purchased wholesale from Bombay; sewing thread is bought at the local market. The producers are paid piece rates based on the complexity of the design.*

this is cut, and the raw edges turned under and stitched. The *molas* are made as rectangular panels; traditionally two of these, one front, one back (the same shape but different patterns), are incorporated into the Cuna women's blouses. A plain – or nowadays brightly printed – cloth is then used for the yoke and sleeves.

Occasionally, Christian symbols such as angels have appeared in the appliqué panels of Panama and Colombia, indicating the presence of missionaries in the region; but more commonly,

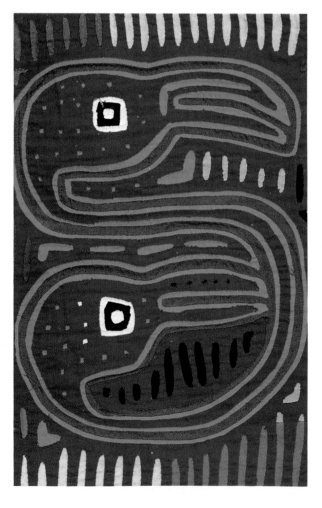

LEFT AND BELOW LEFT: *Two details of* mola *reverse appliqué panels, made by Cuna Indians living in Panama and Colombia. Mostly Cuna women do* mola *work, but occasionally men make these panels too. They are usually made into blouses, over which a moneybox key is often worn by those women who negotiate prices with traders coming into coastal ports, while their husbands are away farming and fishing. Panels are taken off and replaced when the wearer wants a change of design.*

images of birds, humans and plants are featured. The Cuna believe that every creature that lives and every plant that grows is imbued with spirit, and that it is possible to be protected from any evil spirits by drawing an image of that being on one's body in tattoo or painted form. It is generally thought that their embroidery is derived from these forms of body decoration, possibly using the same imagery as that used in the Cuna picture writing, for Cunas have no written word language.

The *mola* is now being made in panels for sale, but though its imagery is traditional, the context of its usage has developed. It is also perceived as a sign of resistance and independence among the indigenous people of Panama. When the Cuna Indian children were expected to conform by wearing Western-style school uniform, rectangles were cut out of the blouses and *molas* defiantly inserted in their place, although the regulation skirt and school colours around the neck and sleeves were retained. The use of this appliqué in machine-made fabrics is now quite widespread – and is almost a kind of badge, for it is also included in Cuna men's sports clothing, and everyday collars and ties.

As far as we know from surviving textiles, appliqué has rarely involved the use of homespun cloths, and today the advantages of crisp, light, polyester-cotton may outweigh any sentiment for the 100% natural – in the producers' eyes, at least. In the Thai hilltribe villages, some groups grow and spin their own yarn, but others are delighted to purchase factory cloth. The rainbow of overlapping strips of manufactured cotton around the yoke and shoulders of Lisu girls' clothing is an example of this fresh approach.

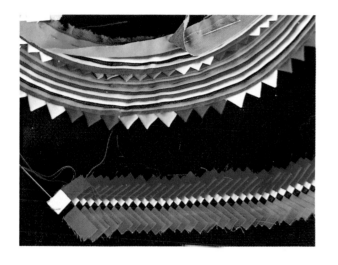

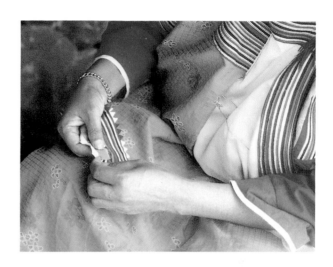

LEFT: *Sample of Lisu appliqué technique, Northern Thailand.*

RIGHT: *Lisu woman wearing traditional dress with appliqué yoke and neck, making a similar garment in a hilltribe village.*

BELOW: *Lisu girls in traditional dress. The Lisu come from China and migrated to Thailand via Burma.*

LEFT: *An* arpillera *from Peru, depicting the harvesting of* tuna (*prickly pears*) *and cochineal insects; made by women now living on the outskirts of Lima. These appliqué pictures are light-hearted in their subject matter, but the craft is based on* arpilleras *with a political message created by Chilean women.*

ABOVE RIGHT: *Detail of appliqué cushion cover made by Aymara Indians living near Sarata, Bolivia. About 100 families are involved: dyeing handspun wool, knitting garments, and creating pictures such as this.*

MESSAGES BEHIND THE MEDIUM

Worked into embroidery – the best examples of which take many hours to make – are emotions, stories passed down from mother to daughter, and all the romance which has become a legendary aspect of the craft. The *arpillera* (meaning "sacking") depicts views of life in Latin America, with (somewhat idealized) images of, for instance, Peruvians harvesting potatoes, cactus fruits and cochineal insects for dyeing. In fact, many producers in Peru now live in urban environments which are the antithesis of the settings they record: colourless shanty settlements on the dusty edge of town, rather than the beautiful Andean countryside where they used to live. Today, Colombian women are also making similar appliqué pictures called *gobelinos*. When asked whether they enjoy and benefit from their work, the answer is double-edged: although they do not necessarily earn more by being in a group, at least

LEFT: *Hmong woman applying small pieces of red machine-made cloth to indigo-dyed batik; Northern Thailand.*

BELOW: *Detail of a Hmong appliqué bedspread in polyester cotton; the whole spread is made up of nearly 100 such squares, each in a different design.*

they have more control over their affairs and any benefits coming their way; besides, they add, it is much nicer to work together.

The act of women embroidering collectively, so that as they discuss their lives, their stories take shape, is nothing new. But each traumatic episode in the history of the producers also proves a catalyst for new forms of expression – such were the origins of the *arpilleras*, in which the harsher side of reality was revealed.

Following the military coup of 1973, when General Pinochet seized power in Chile, the wives and relatives of the "disappeared" took to making appliqué pictures of protest. Composed of patches of old cloth applied to sacking, the activity of making an *arpillera* was an act of solidarity in itself, as women sewed together in self-help groups. Some figures in these pictures had real pieces of paper tucked into their crocheted arms, bearing demands for more milk and medicine, and "Justice Now".

In 1980, two members of the Zamani Soweto Sisters self-help group from South Africa saw an exhibition of Chilean *arpilleras* in London, and were so moved by them that they helped to develop this politicized art form amongst their own people. The embroidered hangings of the Hmong people in Thailand echo too their changing history. In 1975, the Hmong people were forced out of Laos into Thailand. Their embroidered hangings both recall this difficult journey, and celebrate a way of life in rural Laos which they will never see again. Nearly 100,000 Hmong people have since moved on to other countries – most of them are settled in the United States, although some are now resident in Australia, France and French Guyana.

THE FUTURE OF EMBROIDERY

Interestingly, as a result of the Hmong relatives sending a brighter palette of commercially dyed embroidery threads back from California, a number of innovations in colour and texture have now been introduced to the work of embroiderers still living in Thailand. However, worldwide, some fine embroidery work is in danger of being lost forever, partly because traditional threads are no longer available. Producers are increasingly dependent on factory spinners and weavers, and this is changing the character of their work – sometimes for better, sometimes for worse. Western consumers often prefer the figurative to the abstract in embroidery, and so in trying to sell work, there is a tendency for the embroiderers to make recognizable pictures (as in woven tapestries and painted batiks), though more abstract patterns may still feature in the smaller items of embroidery which engender a faster turnover within the market.

This is not a new phenomenon: the craft always has been subject to change. A hundred years ago, the embroidering Mochi caste of Kutch in India worked on leather. Then, as they began to produce wedding canopies for people of the Kathiawar peninsula in Western India, their work moved into the finer domain of silk, on which they continued to practise their *aari* (tambour work) technique, creating linear patterns, sometimes of Persian origin, in fluid contours of chain stitch. Because the designs have precedents in older work, someone new to *aari* work might assume that it has a long history in its current form, but this is not so (though there is still a strong tradition of *aari* work on leather in Rajasthan.)

TOP: *Embroidered chair back from Rajasthan and embroidered leather slippers, made in the Banaskantha region of Northern Gujarat.*

ABOVE: *Curing buffalo hides in Bundar Sindri village, Rajasthan, used for embroidered chair backs, slippers* (jootis), *and saddles.*

Once a skill practised by women for adorning themselves and their families, and a vital asset in a marriage dowry, much embroidery is now made for sale. This is not necessarily negative development as supporters of tradition would like to assert. The independence gained by generating some income of their own has given many women the confidence to express themselves, and has created a renewed sense of their own identity, because very often the producers of these crafts and their skills are valued more highly by outsiders than from within their own community. Therefore, although production for sale profoundly influences the types of embroideries made, as well as their designs and colours, the outside interest in such work might be the vital stimulus needed to keep the craft alive. Whilst embroidery has symbolized abundance and regeneration throughout its rich history, ironically it cannot continue to grow in isolation from the outside world.

FLOOR COVERINGS

KNOTTED PILE CARPETS PROBABLY BEGAN AS IMITATIONS OF ANIMAL PELTS – AS
TODAY'S TIBETAN TIGER RUGS REMIND US. BUT THE INCREDIBLY RICH RANGE OF
PATTERNS MAY NOW INCORPORATE ANYTHING FROM ABSTRACT IMAGES DERIVED
FROM NATURE, TO FIGURATIVE WEAPONS OF WAR. THE WORLD OF
FLOORCOVERINGS REACHES BEYOND THE FINEST OF KNOTTED CARPETS,
TO INCLUDE RUGS OF MUCH MORE HUMBLE ORIGINS. DHURRIES AND COIR
MATTING FROM INDIA, JUTE MATS FROM BANGLADESH, AND *SARAPES* FROM
MEXICO ALL HAVE THEIR OWN SPECIAL QUALITIES, TEXTURES, AND COLOURS.

The original functions of today's floorcoverings, in many cases, were quite different from their current use. The Mexican *sarape*, for instance, began as a man's shoulder blanket. Tibetan tiger rugs were never intended to be walked on, but were hung behind or spread on the spot where persons of rank would sit. Conversely, knotted pile rugs and tapestry-woven dhurries and kelims, from Central and South Asia, are now elevated to the wall in the West, where they may enjoy the status of a higher art form. (Ironically, kelims were in fact originally designed as the rough packaging in which finer carpets were transported.)

In many parts of the world carpets have developed over the centuries into splendid symbols of wealth. The earliest knotted carpet to have survived (400–300 BC) is in The Hermitage Museum in St Petersburg, Russia; it was discovered beneath the impacted Siberian ice at a site called Pazyryk. It is extremely fine, with a decorative border depicting men on horseback and saddlebags – possibly themselves made of knotted pile.

ABOVE: *Rug of hand-spun wool; Wollo region, Ethiopia. Common motifs are the Ethiopian cross, churches, lions and birds, diamonds and triangles.*

OPPOSITE: *Mrs Kamla holding up a* panja *dhurry in Balwari village in the north of Haryana state, close to the Punjab border in India – a farming community in which women are restricted in how much they are allowed to move around.*

OPPOSITE, BORDER: *Jute matting from Bangladesh.*

There was a period in the West when the greatest luxury was to own an oriental carpet on which to rest one's feet. In a number of Italian Renaissance paintings, this privilege is conferred on the Madonna, whose throne is placed on a fine knotted pile rug of Turkish or Caucasian origin. Nowadays, some kind of floorcovering, however basic, is found in houses throughout the world. Where reeds, bamboos, or large tropical leaves are available, for example, these may be woven into sleeping mats. A common arrangement in rural South East Asia is for the mat to be placed on a raised bamboo platform which doubles up as the cooking area of the house during the day.

METHODS AND MEANS

The creation of floorcoverings involves techniques shared with several other craft products, especially baskets and woven textiles. Tapestry weaving and twining techniques are employed to make the flat-woven rugs of cotton and/or wool in Ethiopia, India, Bangladesh, Peru and elsewhere. For extra warmth and comfort, rows of tufts may be knotted between every second or third passage of weft, to create a pile. There are many ways of tying a knot around the warp (vertical) threads of the carpet, and some, like the Tibetan, can be traced to their place of origin by the particular knot used. The number of knots per square centimetre affects the amount of detail achievable: more knots are used for finer rugs, and fewer are used for coarser rugs. Felting, by contrast, is a non-woven technique practised in many parts of Asia including Kashmir in Northern India, whereby the wool fibres are arranged randomly and are then encouraged by heat, moisture, and pressure, to cling to one another.

Frequently, the techniques involved in the making of floor coverings, and the materials employed in their creation, complement other crafts of the area. Thus producers living in tropical regions, such as the Htin people of Northern Thailand, the Chachi Indians of Ecuador, and the T'Boli on Mindanao island in the Southern Philippines, all weave mats with exactly the same patterns, techniques and plant materials as they use for making baskets. The abundant fibre of Bangladesh, jute, is used for woven dhurries as well as knotted mesh hammocks and *sikas* (hanging baskets).

Available materials affect the style and function of a piece, too. The Indian dhurry, though usually made of cotton, has sometimes been made of silk or wool, according to the climate of the region and status of the user. Ethiopian floor-coverings are made from undyed wool of the short-tailed highland sheep, whose natural fleece colour ranges from creamy-white to darkest brown. Kashmir in the Himalayas is the home of the *namdhas*, embroidered felt rugs which make economic use of the shorter-stapled, lower quality wool left over from shawl weaving.

TOP RIGHT: *Sorting out and fluffing up fleece in Kashmir, India.*

MIDDLE RIGHT: *Spreading out the damp fleece on a mat, ready to be rolled.*

BOTTOM RIGHT: *Tracing the* namdha *design onto felt.*

OPPOSITE, TOP LEFT: *Detail of a* namdha, *an embroidered felt rug from Kashmir, India.*

OPPOSITE, TOP RIGHT: *Embroidering a* namdha.

OPPOSITE, BOTTOM: *Washing* namdhas *in Dal Lake, Srinagar, Kashmir.*

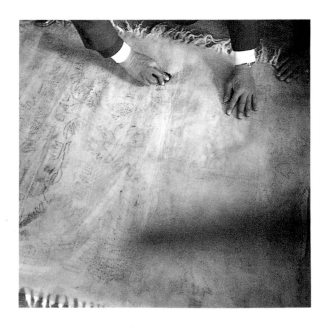

PATTERNS OF WAR

Afghan refugees are now producing pile carpets at Akora Khattak camp in Pakistan. There are two stylistic traditions represented: the Baluchi and the Turkoman, based on different tribal patterns. They all work with a distinctive colour range of dark brick-red and deepest indigo, with smaller highlights of white. In the past, when these people's ancestors led a more peripatetic existence, their carpets in fact included many more colours. Part of the appeal of rugs made by nomadic peoples lies in the subtle variation of colour and tone; as they tended to dye their yarn in small batches, an unevenness of hue inevitably resulted. When Turkoman tribespeople began a more settled life in Afghanistan during the later 19th century, their palette became more limited. This is partly because they were able to dye larger quantities of yarn, resulting in a uniform shade across the carpet, and partly because by the 1880s a limited colour range of synthetic (aniline) dyes was available in Central Asia. By that date, they were facing competition from machine-woven imitations of their rugs produced in Europe, and had to standardize patterns in order to meet the orders from European carpet dealers. For these weavers, as for the factories, it saved time and money to restrict the colour range.

Since witnessing the fighting which occurred during the Soviet military occupation of Afghanistan (1979–1989), when their homes and villages were destroyed, some refugees have been expressing new observations in the pictorial form most natural to them. At first glance these "Baluchi"-style carpets resemble conventional abstract designs, but a closer look reveals that they

OPPOSITE: Detail of Afghan war carpet. Some of the teenage men who are now carpet trainees in Akora Khattak camp could hardly have remembered the impact of the Soviet invasion of Afghanistan; yet these war carpets are being produced more than 13 years after the event.

RIGHT: View of Akora Khattak refugee camp. The camp, where carpets are being woven by 40 Kandhari people, is one of many in the North West Frontier Province of Pakistan, some distance from Peshawar. The bleakness of the desert landscape seems to make the richness of the carpet patterns that much more meaningful. The creations become the flowers of the desert, and through them a sense of heritage can be passed down.

now contain silhouettes of machine-guns, military tanks, and aeroplanes – chilling echoes of the old motifs which they have replaced. It is a sad irony that traumatic military intervention should jolt carpet design into fresh imagery. The traditional medallion carpets based on Turkoman models are still being produced, and are popular in the marketplace, but their more coded images may appear bland alongside Baluchi images of war.

CARPETS OF TIBET

Another group of people from a famous carpet-making tradition, who as refugees are dependent on a living from it, are the Tibetans exiled in Nepal and India since 1959. Since then, the

LEFT: *Weaving a typical Tibetan design, India.*

RIGHT: *Trimming a Tibetan carpet for a low-relief effect.*

production of hand-knotted carpets has helped the Tibetans to generate income and maintain some symbols of their cultural identity, for carpets represent 80% of the Tibetans' craft output. The quantity produced varies considerably from one refugee centre to another: some of the settlements in India, located in old tea plantations and woollen mills, weave a thousand or more per year; a monastery on the other hand might produce only a few. In India, production is centrally organized with the support of the Tibetan government-in-exile; Tibetan weavers in Nepal are, however, mostly working for private enterprises, who capitalize on the country's thriving tourist industry.

Traditionally, the Tibetan pile carpet had many variations in the tightness of its weave and number of knots per centimetre, each type suiting a different household use – sleeping bags, for example, were made of a relatively light and flexible pile fabric compared to the more densely knotted carpets. Designs were – and still are – equally varied, and the weavers adapt styles and

colours to suit the requirements of different markets. Vases, fretwork, and "wave" borders are typical and popular motifs, the rug contours of which may be clipped for a low-relief effect. Woven with a deep blue background, this type is favoured by Tibetan patrons; Western taste prefers muted pastel colours (vegetable-dyed, if possible). Indian customers, on the other hand, tend to enjoy the rich effects of different tones in the same colour.

The majority of designs are drawn from an existing decorative vocabulary. Buddhist symbols are deeply sacred, and strictly speaking must not be sat, slept, or stood upon, although they have for years been incorporated as purely decorative motifs and stood upon by Westerners. A more unusual case was a carpet commissioned by one German patron. It involved copying in its entirety a 4-metre square painting of a mandala by the master of the Thangka School, for which the patron had to receive written permission from His Holiness the Dalai Lama, the Tibetans' Leader-in-Exile.

LEFT: *Some tiger rugs, like this one, were obviously originally imitations of pelts; others have developed into purely abstract patterns of stripes with no pictorial element.*

The Tibetan tiger rug is a bit of an enigma. No-one is sure of its origins, though it was probably an object of status, as this animal symbolized rank and power. One photograph from the 1920s shows a local Mongol chief seated in judgement on a Tibetan rug, with a tiger rug hung behind him; another from the 1930s records a former Tibetan Minister of Agriculture seated on a tiger skin. The rug probably began as a substitute for real pelts, and may have been used by members of secret Tantric religious sects as well as persons of political authority, to sit on during lengthy periods of meditation or meetings of state. It was also used in dances during Tibetan New Year celebrations.

In any case, the tiger rugs no longer have such mystical or ceremonial connotations. For some time no-one was making them, but production was revived just a few years ago, in response to the immense interest shown in an exhibition held in London. *The Tiger Rugs of Tibet* featured 108 old rugs – an auspicious number in Tibetan culture, for a Tibetan girl's hair is arranged in 108 plaits, and there are as many volumes in the Lamaic scripture. Although some rugs are very obviously imitations of tiger skins, others have developed into a complex pattern of stripes with no pictorial element.

FROM SHOULDER TO FLOOR

During the past century, as interest in American Indian handicrafts has grown, shoulder "blankets" – once ceremonial garments – have undergone all kinds of adaptations so that they become suitable for use on the floor. This is true of Hopi and Navajo weaving in Arizona and New Mexico

as well as of the *sarape*, a feature of Mexican national dress for men. Typically, the *sarape* swathes the body over one arm across to the opposite shoulder, and looks most dashing when the wearer is on horseback. In the past, some of these Mexican blankets were trimmed with silk braid down the sides, and fringes at each end. Today's are mostly woven in bright acrylic, the fluorescence appealing to local taste.

As a garment, the *sarape* may have derived from the pre-Spanish Conquest "capes of 100 colours" (*centzontilmatli*), which were eye-dazzlingly bright, with their patterns of zig-zags and diamonds – also characteristic of today's rugs. In the mid-19th century, an Englishman by the name of Sir Edward B. Tylor published his description of a journey across Mexico made during a lull in the civil disturbances. In his book *Anahuac: or Mexico and the Mexicans, Ancient and Modern*, he described the blanket:

> ". . . wider than the Scotch plaid . . . and woven in some gaudy Oriental patterns which are to be seen on the prayer-carpets of Turkey and Palestine to this day. It is worn as a cloak . . . muffling up half the face when its owner is chilly or does not wish to be recognized. When a heavy rain comes down, and he is on horseback, he puts his head through the slit in the middle, and becomes a moving tent. At night he rolls himself up in it, and sleeps on a mat or a board, or on the stones in the open air . . ."

At the same time as "orientalizing" the design, the Mexican blanket made the transition from shoulder to floor. A number of today's blankets produced for the Western market are of cotton and wool, heavier and coloured with natural dyes.

ABOVE: *Detail of a* sarape, *made by weavers in Teotitlan del Valle, Mexico.*

BELOW: *Detail of Indian* panja dhurry, *from Haryana state, near the Punjab border; woven by women in the villages.*

OPPOSITE: *Ratni Devi, a* panja *dhurry weaver from Mayon village, Haryana, India. The term* panja *(meaning five) refers to the heavy comb used to beat the wefts in place, which originally had five teeth – like an extension to the hand.*

DHURRIES DISCOVERED

The Indian dhurry is a flat rug, usually of cotton, which comes in many sizes, designs and degrees of fineness. All types are tapestry-woven, though there are subtle differences of texture, and in the methods of switching from one colour to the next. Although the craft is mostly associated with Northern India, dhurries are being woven all around the country; some are produced in urban workshops by men, others by women in their rural homes. According to the region and various circumstances of production, a different type of loom is used.

The tradition goes back several centuries, during which the dhurry has been used in three principal ways. Bed dhurries made of thick cotton are used in Indian homes. Usually hidden from sight because they are sandwiched between the wooden frame of the bed and the mattress. Today, this type is usually power-woven in India's mills.

The second use is for prayer. These dhurries vary according to Muslim or Hindu customs. The Muslim ones are often woven in long strips – in effect a series of panels (*saphs*), each of which is woven with the shape of an Islamic arch (representing the *mihrab* niche or slab in the mosque, indicating the direction of Mecca, towards which all worshippers pray), and maybe a mosque lamp; these prayer mats can be shared. The Hindu prayer dhurry (*asan*), on the other hand, singles out the worshipper, for it serves to retain his purity; following the ritualistic ablution, he must avoid contamination from others while he prays.

More familiar in the West, the third type of dhurry is for the floor. These can be quite small;

but for special celebrations, can also be of vast proportions. Sometimes the design imitates ceramic floor tiles, but in effect, anything and everything has been woven into these floorcoverings, from traditional Indian designs to Victorian cabbage roses. The dhurry has been responsive to diverse demands, from the Mughal emperors to British military officers, and now tourist hotels and export markets.

COIR MATTING

Probably the greatest production of tufted coconut fibre mats is in Kerala, a state on the South Western coast of India where coconut palms abound. The tree *Cocos nucifera* has been known and used in India for at least 3000 years. Today it provides the leaves for weaving a wide range of practical items from sleeping-mats to baskets, as well as the flesh for eating and palm oil, toddy sap for fermenting and distilling the local palm wine and mind-blowing arrack (otherwise known as "fire water"), and coir (pronounced "coya").

The coir fibres, which form a protective layer between the smooth shell of the coconut fruit and the white flesh are extremely resilient. Coir is the only fibre naturally resistant to sea water. It is extremely tough, due to its high lignin content, but rather unbending because of this, and consequently physically exacting to work with. The age of fibres affects the way they function: darker ones are stronger because they are more mature, but the lighter ones are more flexible. Coconuts are picked from the trees at regular intervals — a precarious job, because the men risk their lives climbing the tall, slender tree trunks to reach the coconuts at the top. Many trees will yield around

ABOVE: *River transport by the coir works, Shertallai Mats and Matting Co-operative Society. The Society has around 200–300 registered members, of whom only around a dozen are women. Wages are paid on a piece rate, each section (spooling, dyeing, weaving, and so on) being paid at a different rate. Hand-operated technology dating from 1850 is still being used.*

RIGHT: *Coir drying in Shertallai, Kerala state, South India.*

FAR RIGHT: *Detail of coir woven matting.*

80 coconuts per year, though a 200-year old one may produce 250 fruits.

Once picked, the coconut is de-husked by jamming the fruit onto a stake to remove the outer shell and reveal the fibrous layer beneath. The coir fibres are then soaked for up to 10 months in pits or nets, in slow-moving water, in order to swell and soften them. They are dried, beaten with a wooden mallet against the ground, and separated into shorter coir for mattresses and upholstery padding, and longer bristles for weaving mats. (This is the material from which our traditional doormat is made.)

The production of coir floorcoverings was established in Kerala state in the mid-19th century – and the heavy man-operated looms have not changed since. Beating, spinning and weaving coir are laborious processes, and are not well rewarded – especially for women, whose activities in the preparation of fibre earn them less than a quarter of a master weaver's rate.

Despite all this there is nonetheless some resistance to change in the coir production industry.

The back-breaking tasks involved in coir production could be made lighter, but to update the looms would be an extremely costly enterprise, particularly as it would require specialized machinery. Improved technology would certainly mean job losses for a good proportion of the half-million Indians working in coir processing and production.

BELOW: *Raksha winding thread onto spools ready for weaving a dhurry, in Kardhan village, Haryana state, North India.*

PAST, PRESENT, AND FUTURE

Although some hand-woven products have been superseded by factory goods – notably carpets by the metre, and the bed dhurries of India which are of standardized dimensions – the appeal of an individual piece of design still holds. It is encouraging to learn that many weavers new to the

LEFT: *Dhurry, woven by a group of skilled craftsmen near Jodhpur, Rajasthan.*

RIGHT: *Detail of an Inca calendar executed in Ayacucho-style tapestry weaving, from Peru. Their pre-Columbian heritage is very important to today's craft producers in Latin America, partly for cultural reasons, partly because this is what customers look for.*

craft of making floorcoverings are taking a fresh approach. For instance, while the Indian government programme of handicraft revival has grown since the 1950s, more interest has been shown in the dhurry's potential, both within India and in the West. Accordingly, as more weavers receive training in design and technique, their confidence grows, and with it, their skills and their imaginative representations of the world around them.

As the latest Indian dhurries, Tibetan tiger rugs, Afghan war carpets, and Mexican *sarapes* testify, traditions are lost and found, and are constantly reinterpreted. In so doing, they reflect late 20th-century encounters which, looking back, will prove to be turning points in design and craft production. The catalysts are extraordinarily different: as we have seen, they include the market place, the desperate need for income, the art gallery, and the front line.

RECYCLING

FOREVER RESPONSIVE TO PRACTICAL AND DECORATIVE NEEDS, PEOPLE ROUND
THE WORLD HAVE RECYCLED AND REUSED MATERIALS, EITHER FOR THEIR OWN
USE, OR FOR THE EVENTUAL BENEFIT OF ANOTHER GENERATION OR SECTOR OF
SOCIETY. THIS IS AS TRUE OF REMOTER AREAS LIKE MINDANAO IN THE PHILIPPINES
AS IT IS OF URBAN ENVIRONMENTS WITH NO NATURAL MATERIALS, SUCH AS
PORT-AU-PRINCE, HAITI. ADMIRED AND ENJOYED FOR THEIR INVENTIVENESS,
THESE CRAFT OBJECTS NOW APPEAL FOR AN ADDITIONAL REASON –
ENVIRONMENTAL CONCERN OVER THE FUTURE OF RESOURCES.

[C]elebrating the resourceful ways in which people transform waste materials into attractive and serviceable objects seems an appropriate conclusion to this book. In all crafts – from pots to papermaking – the initial stimulus to be creative is conditioned by the resources available. In developing countries "availability" means, amongst other things, "affordable" by those people who depend on crafts for a living. Whether pre-consumed rejects of industry or worn-out clothing, waste materials are usually cheaper, and so an obvious source of material.

Making something beautiful out of nothing continues to be a challenge, especially in the developing world. Inventive products today include crocheted hats from Lesotho and *sikas* from Bangladesh made out of plastic strips; melted-down plastic combs, brass carburettors and taps, reformed into jewellery and figurines by the T'Boli people in the Philippines; and, in Haiti, painted Caribbean-style buses and houses made out of cement-bag papier mâché – or of beaten metal cut-outs from disused oil drums.

ABOVE: *Hat made from plastic bags, being sold in a Lesotho market, Southern Africa.*

OPPOSITE: *Metal painter, Haiti, holding a spray-painted snake cut out from an old oil drum.*

OPPOSITE, BORDER: *Detail of* chindi *(rags), from Ahmedabad, India. Thousands of women and children in Indian cities depend for their livelihood on collecting litter of all types for recycling.*

WASTE NOT

Sometimes this necessity of re-use is incorporated in the customs and belief systems of society. In many Hindu and Buddhist communities, for example, the act of patching is a sign of humility, the example being set by religious ascetics, rag gods, and the Buddha himself. The creation of something whole from separate, worn parts is also deeply significant. The *kanthas* of Bangladesh, and the similar embroidered quilts of Bihar and West Bengal, were traditionally made from scraps and unpicked threads of worn-out saris and dhotis. *Kanthas* are presented as gifts on special occasions such as marriage. Regenerated from old materials, they express far more than a gift that is new.

The sorting and sale of *chindi* (rags) is integral to the Indian textile industry and to the Hindu caste system, in which designated groups of *chindi* pickers sort the bundles according to quality and size. The main source of *chindi* is Ahmedabad in Gujarat, a city of textile mills, where rags are recycled into second-grade textile goods, mostly for the local market, some (such as rag rugs) for

export. The waste from Ahmedabad's textile industry has given rise to a whole sub-economy. Contractors purchase the unusable scraps of odd-shaped and oil-stained cloth and sell it by weight to women who make *chindi* quilts, known as *khols*; these, though dirty from the outset, are used by the city's poor.

But the picking and use of waste does not stop there, for through all of India's cities and many smaller towns there are thousands of women and children roaming the streets, gathering litter – paper, plastic bags, polythene sheets, bottles, scrap iron and other discarded materials – which will be recycled into many kinds of goods for eventual use by all strata of society. Absolutely nothing is permitted to go to total waste. Not only are these waste products reused on a large manu-

ABOVE: *Rag rugs, from Varanasi, India.*

LEFT: *Women sorting out various qualities of rags, Ahmedabad, India.*

RIGHT: *Cleaning and finishing rag rugs. The producers of these rag rugs live in Varanasi, though most rags* (chindi) *come from Ahmedabad, the Gujarati city of textile mills where* chindi *forms the basis of a whole sub-economy. Most rug makers are Muslims, weaving at home on* panja *looms.*

facturing scale, but discarded objects sometimes become the tools of family-based craft workshops; rusting iron is used for dyeing cloth, and items such as tin lids are used for scraping bamboo cane to make the coiled bowls hung in the *sikas* of Bangladesh.

In Thailand fabric scraps are similarly re-used, made into jaunty oven gloves and toys to generate income. And on a purely decorative note, the women there who tend the silk moths have found a new use for silk cocoons. Those which are not reeled for their precious thread, but are left alone for the moths to hatch, can later be dyed in bright shades and transformed into fluorescent bunches of flowers.

Most items are recycled from locally used goods. However, sometimes the desire or need

for a certain raw material has obliged people to "de-make" a craft before they can make something new. In the 19th century, some American Indian weavers re-used dyed English woollen baize (*bayeta*), in order to get particular colours. Red was especially highly prized: in Arizona and New Mexico it was used sparingly in the Navajo's striped "chieftain" blankets, where it stood out from the deep indigo blue and undyed cream and dark brown shades of their local sheep's wool. Today, in the Afghan refugee camps of Pakistan, the use of unravelled goods is neither so selective, nor so prestigious; but the results are extremely colourful and practical. To produce patterned slipper-socks, second-hand knitted sweaters are bought by the truck-load from the market at Peshawar, and unpicked for their yarn.

ABOVE: *Slipper socks ready to be sent to Oxfam Trading. The slippers have to be sorted and sized before despatch from Peshawar, Pakistan. Around 15,000 families live in Jelozia camp, about 300 of whom are involved in the slipper sock knitting project. Ockenden Venture, a UK-based refugee agency, provides bales of second-hand sweaters purchased in the bazaar. Women unravel them and knit the yarn into socks and gloves, working on average for 5–6 hours per day; the men then sew on the soles.*

RIGHT: *Various festival decorations are made from cotton scraps by Srinivas Malliah Memorial Theatre Crafts, Delhi, India.*

LEFT: *A metal painter, Haiti, painting a house cut out from an old oil drum.*

BELOW: *A painted bus and Caribbean-style painted tin house made from recycled oil drums; Haiti. Employment is minimal in Haiti, and tourism non-existent; but the painted products of recycled items are now being marketed to other Caribbean islands as well as the United States. There is much artistic talent in Haiti: graffiti and paintings appear on walls and local buses are brightly painted with religious figures and folk heroes.*

Metal, too, is put to artistic use. Perhaps the most striking and witty examples of this are the painted cut-outs of Caribbean buses and houses, made from flattened, disused oil drums. These items have become so popular that the Haitians are even importing old cans from the United States, to keep up with demand (they are then sold back to the Americans). In the Philippines, the T'Boli people do not beat out, but melt down their metal: old brass taps, carburettors and ashtrays. From these, they make elaborate figurines and chain belts with bells, using the lost-wax modelling technique, whereby the mould for casting the metal is formed around a wax model which then melts away.

Plastic is also being recycled by the T'Boli people, who produce a range of jewellery from melted-down rulers, set squares, combs and other

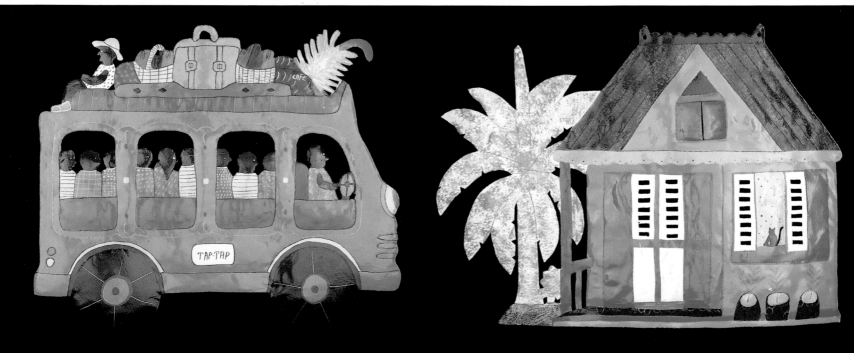

LEFT: *Figure made from recycled brass by the T'Boli people of Mindanao island, Philippines.*

BELOW LEFT: *Melted plastic jewellery made by the T'Boli (originally they made necklaces of glass beads, obtained from the Muslim traders on the island). Also shown is a rolled paper necklace made out of old magazines by Peruvian women living on the outskirts of Lima.*

which takes dye well, and which is everywhere. Glitter is frequently added to this.

In Peru, a group of women living on the outskirts of Lima are creating necklaces which require close scrutiny to discover the source of their materials. They cut up old magazines into strips barely more than a millimetre wide, and painstakingly coil them into beads. And in Thailand, tightly rolled and varnished newspaper is being made into exquisite miniature baskets, sold through some tourist markets.

ENVIRONMENT-FRIENDLY

Such inventiveness on the part of producers in the developing world, though based on extreme necessity, is admired in the West for ecological reasons. One measurement of value which is new is the Western attitude towards re-using, re-cycling, and mending, not simply out of necessity, but for ethical correctness. In the early 1990s, thrift is gradually becoming regarded not as dowdy or mean, but responsible. The transformation of waste into new products has taken on a moral aesthetic to be admired, whilst also appealing for its novelty value. It can perhaps be seen as part of Western societies' last-ditch attempt to check the rate at which the world's natural resources are being diminished.

For many of the craftspeople concerned, it is difficult to comprehend why a discarded object should become fashionable and highly desirable. For example, in January 1992 one family-run workshop producing miniature *retablos* in Peru was found to be setting the figurines in chewing-gum packets. When it was suggested that they should give up the practice of painting the packet

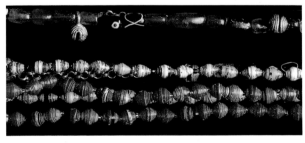

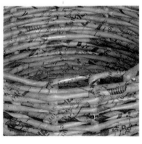

brightly coloured items. (Some combs escape the fire, for they are much admired as hair ornaments – the bigger the better, and worn with panache.) Further north in the Philippines, in Olongapo where the big American naval base is located, other income-generation projects also include the making of jewellery. Earrings have been made with sand and wire, set in a synthetic resin; but since the eruption of Mount Pinatubo, the producers have begun to use the volcanic ash

ABOVE: *Detail of basket made from newspaper strips wrapped around wire; made by a group in Nonthaburi, Thailand. Newspaper is recycled for all sorts of uses.*

INDEX

FURTHER READING

There are a number of books available on particular craft traditions in the countries featured in *World Crafts*, which may be found in larger libraries and bookshops.

If you would like to learn more about Oxfam's work in these countries, or about the fair trade movement, here are some starting points.

Adams, Richard, *Who Profits?* (the story of Traidcraft). Lion Press, 1989.

Black, Maggie, *A Cause for Our Time: Oxfam – The First 50 Years*. Oxford University Press/ Oxfam, 1992.
Coote, Belinda, *The Trade Trap: Poverty and the Global Commodity Markets*. Oxfam, 1992.
Davidson, Joan, and Myers, Dorothy, with Chakraborty, Manab, *No Time to Waste: Poverty and the Global Environment*. Oxfam, 1992.
Oxfam Country Brief Series, The, including *Bangladesh: The Strength to Succeed, India:*

Paths to Development, Vietnam: The Price of Peace, and *Zimbabwe: A Land Divided*.
Oxfam 50: Our World in Photographs. Collins and Brown, 1992.
Wells, Phil, and Jetter, Mandy, *The Global Consumer*. Victor Gollancz, 1991.

Oxfam books are available from: Oxfam Publications, 274 Banbury Road, Oxford OX2 7DZ.

ACKNOWLEDGEMENTS

The author would like to thank the following individuals and organizations:
I am indebted to all the staff at Oxfam Trading's Bridge office, who have shared their knowledge and experiences of fieldwork, and who in so doing have allowed me the privilege of a particularly detailed insight into Bridge. Many thanks to buying staff Carol Wills, Liz Mann and Edward Millard, who have given up precious time to answer questions, and especially to information staff Emma Gough, Rachel Wilshaw and Tracy Adamson, who have spent hours talking this project through, and feeding me with information, support and photographs – without which this book would not have happened.

I would like to thank the producer groups in Africa, Asia and Latin America who have supplied information about the people and skills, who are both the subject of and the reason for this book. However, I would also like to mention Oxfam Trading's overseas representatives: Martín Barragán, Mathew Cherian, Darwin Flores, Julie George, Mohammad Islam, Amita Joseph, David Newell, Sudhir Rao, Renuka, Emily Ryan and Bonar Saragih.

Several friends deserve acknowledgement for generously sharing their expertise: Patricia Baker, Jenny Balfour-Paul, Linda Brassington, Susan Conway, Jill and Keith Nicklin, Sally Reid, Shuna Rendell, Nigel Wood and, last but not least, Janet Rogers for allowing me to read her Royal College of Art MA report (1990) on the practice of design and marketing of handcrafts produced in developing countries.

Cortina Butler of Letts Publishers and Robert Cornford of Oxfam initiated the idea for *World Crafts*; I am grateful to them, and to Joanna Lorenz, Editorial Director at Anness Publishing, for the opportunity to write this book and for their tremendous help and advice.

The author and publishers would like to thank the following Oxfam staff for supplying photographs for this book:
John Ballyn, David Bettle, Tony Brayshaw, Liz Clayton, Robert M. Davis, Ben Fawcett, Emma Gough, Patsy Hughes, Caroline Lucas, Peter McCulloch, Edward Millard, Tricia Parker, David Newell, Ray Stringer, Carol Wills, Rachel Wilshaw, Pat Wise.

The author and publishers would also like to thank the following for their kind permission to reproduce photographs in this book:
Asia Crafts, India; Badal; Bangladesh Rural Advancement Committee; Bridget Crampton; Nigel Crofton; Nancy Durrell-McKenna; Julio Etchart; Mike Goldwater; Ana-Cecilia Gonzales; Jeremy Hartley; Jimmy Holmes; Vanessa Keegan; Minka, Peru; Neota, India; Ross Payne; Marion Pocock; Pushpanjali, India; Sarvodaya, Sri Lanka; Kathy Sharp; Sasha, India; Rajendra Shaw; Christine Sherringham; Viji Srinivasan; Urmul Trust, India; Mike Wells.